How to Read
A
Cash Flow Statement

Finance Made Easy Series

Financial success is the *raison d'être* of any business, and financial health of any organization is reflected in its financial statements. But it has been observed that managerial professionals often have inadequate understanding of finance and little time to read treatises on it. Further, financial statements are regarded as too complex to understand and left to be 'deciphered' by financial experts. Hence, cultivating a culture of awareness and transparency of finance is a prime imperative.

Finance Made Easy Series has been designed to impart management executives with adequate knowledge to understand and appreciate financial statements and their implications for the fiscal solvency of their firms. This series seeks to demystify apparently complex financial statements, and help create a finance-savvy executive class, the key to fiscally sound and successful businesses. A lucid, creative and concise exposition of financial statements—their components, jargons and computational methods—with short stories and numerical examples makes for engaging reading for busy professionals.

Titles in the series:

- How to Read a Balance Sheet
- How to Read a Profit and Loss Statement
- How to Read a Cash Flow Statement
- How to Analyze Financial Statements

How to Read A Cash Flow Statement

Second Edition

N. Ramachandran

Director of Kochi Business School, Kochi, Kerala

Ram Kumar Kakani

Professor, XLRI – Xavier School of Management, Jamshedpur, India

McGraw Hill Education (India) Private Limited

Published by McGraw Hill Education (India) Private Limited,
Anjana Complex No: 5/90 A, Butt Road, St. Thomas Mount, Chennai – 600016, Tamil Nadu, India.

How to Read a Cash Flow Statement, 2e

Fifteenth reprint 2025

Print Edition:
ISBN-13: 978-93-5134-301-1
ISBN-10: 93-5134-301-4

Ebook Edition
ISBN-13: 978-93-5134-302-8
ISBN-10: 93-5134-302-2

16 17 18 19 20 SAN 29 28 27 26 25

Typeset at Script Makers, 19, A1-B, DDA Market, Paschim Vihar, New Delhi 110 063 and printed and bound in India at Sanat Printers, 312, EPIP, HSIDC, Kundli, Sonepat, Haryana

Cover Design: Kapil Gupta

Visit us at: www.mheducation.co.in
Toll free in India: 1800 103 5875
Write to us at: support.india@mheducation.com
CIN: U80302TN2010PTC111532

Preface

Financial success is arguably the primary purpose around which all management business activities revolve. In order to build an economically viable company, the employees in all departments, need to understand the financial ramifications of their action on the overall fiscal health of the organization. For this to happen, it is very important that not only finance managers, but managers in all other fields too have an adequate knowledge of the subject. The pervasiveness of such knowledge could ultimately help differentiate a successful organization from a bankrupt one. Most of us will remember this dialogue from the movie *Jerry Maguire*, "Show me the money!" Financial statements do exactly the same, they show us how and from where a company's money flows in, where it goes, and what is its present situation.

There are three main financial statements, of which two have already been discussed in the first two books of Finance Made Easy Series-2/e, i.e. "*How to Read a Balance Sheet-2/e*" and "*How to Read a Profit and Loss Statement-2/e*". In this book, we will be elucidating on the "Cash Flow Statement".

The series of books, *Finance Made Easy Series*, has been written for management executives, to impart the knowledge required in order to understand the basic financial statements. *The Finance Made Easy Series* is an attempt to break the myth that financial statements such as the Income Statement, Cash Flow Statement and Balance Sheet are too complex to comprehend.

This particular book deals with Cash Flow Statement. It is by looking at this statement that companies' gauge their actual liquidity position and the financial planning required for maintaining the same. This statement informs the company of regular movements in its funds, allowing it to manage daily functions more efficiently.

Therefore, it becomes imperative for the key decision-makers of a business to have at least rudimentary knowledge about the cash flow statement, and its impact on the business. It is with this confidence that we claim that this book will help you to appreciate the company's fund flow better. We hope readers will appreciate the simple language in which this book is written to reduce all the unnecessary jargons and present the concepts in a lucid format.

NEELAKANTAN RAMACHANDRAN

RAM KUMAR KAKANI

Acknowledgments

Our peers at ICAI, IIM, IIT, XLRI, LBSNAA, SPJIMR and other academic organizations have continuously inspired our thinking. Our research associates have immensely contributed to the manuscript development of this book. We are indebted to:

- Shri Awadesh Jha, Vice President, Moser Baer
- Shri Dushyant Nariala, L.L.B, IAS
- Ms. Nidhi Sharma, PGDBM, PGP-PMP, IRS
- Shri Rajjog Singh, Ph.D.
- Ms. Ranjana Chopra, BA, M.Sc, L.L.B, IAS
- Ms. Shaniya Khanam, B.Sc., MBA
- Ms. Tooshima Sarkar, B.A., M.A.

We are also thankful to Shakti, Jasram Dashmana, Ajay Sharma and Brijesh Bisht for their inspiration, support and feedback.

We would like to thank, Priyanka Goel, Sindhu Ullas, Smita Kulshreshth and other team members of McGraw Hill Professional. In particular, we thank Neha Sharma, whose skillful persuasion and editorial work helped clarify and steady our work enormously.

Finally, we are very grateful to our family members, including Ananya, Aruna, Chinku, Dhruva Govind, Kannan, Karuna, Kriti, Kunju, Lakhpat Rai Goel, Leena, Rathi and Vipra. Thank you all!

Comments from readers are most welcome (Email: ramkumarkakani @gmail.com).

NEELAKANTAN RAMACHANDRAN

RAM KUMAR KAKANI

Contents

Preface *v*
Acknowledgements *vi*

Introduction **1**

1. Funds **3**
Funds *3*
Operating cycle *4*

2. Working Capital **6**
Working Capital *6*
Flow of Funds *7*
Need for Working Capital *8*
Reconciling Increase in Working Capital *14*

3. Capital Invested in Business **15**
Need to Invest in Cash *15*
Need to Invest in Receivables *16*
Need to Invest in Inventory *17*
Need to Invest in Fixed (Non-Current) Assets *18*
Determining the Working Capital Requirement *19*
Future Capital Requirements *21*
Possible Sources of Working Capital *24*
Internal Sources *25*
External sources *27*

4. **Factors Affecting Fund Requirements** **28**

5. **Fund Flow Statement** **34**
The Funds Flow Equations *34*
The Format *35*
Funds Flow from Operations *35*
Statement of Changes in the Working Capital *39*
Changes in the Financial Position *43*
Fund Flow Statement Illustrated *44*

6. **Preparing a Cash Flow Statement** **48**
Format *48*
Preparing Cash Flow Statement: An Introduction *49*

7. **Interpretation of Cash Flow Statement** **58**
The Need for a Cash Flow Statement *64*
Cash and Cash Equivalents *65*

8. **Solved illustrations** **71**
Summary *83*

Exercises **85**
Keys *90*

Index *95*

Introduction

In business, ***Cash*** is referred to as the trump card for any business entity. Employees, suppliers, investors all need to be paid lest a business operation will grind to a halt. Cash is just like the oil in the machine of a business, and a Cash Flow Statement is the just like the cash summary of the machine, wherein all the cash inflows and outflows in a business over a period of time are stated, registering how much cash is available in a business to keep the business running.[1]

Before we move on to have a good discussion on the *Cash Flow Statement*, let us have a look on interesting news.

> **"From Boo To Boo Hoo Hoo ..."**
>
> "Online retailer Boo.com bites the dust" is the screaming headlines of most pink papers and dailies. This was one of the biggest e-tailing failures to hit Europe. Cash flow problems are the stated reasons for the mishap. Losses kept on mounting despite the rising sales. The company filed for bankruptcy, when it failed to raise another round of funding. A classic liquidity trap!
>
> Most dot com companies in the gung-ho days (1999-2000) assumed that venture capitalists, angels, banks and others, would continue to bankroll losses in the name of building the business. The problems came, when the cash tap dried.
>
> The question is, why did the taps dry? What has happened in the recent months that have made investors wary? The answer is - any finance student will tell you that Cash Flow is the way to value. And this never happened for Boo.com again...

What do we see above?

In the above case, we observe that a cash crunch has led to business failure. Another interesting thing to observe is the fact, that there appears to be no

[1]Thus, a Cash Flow Forecast is an estimate, made by the business, of the cash it expects to receive over a period and spend, depending on the progress of the business during that time.

real issues regarding the sales or the future prospects of the company. The crux of the problem lies in handling of the cash flow by the management of these types of companies. Thus, if you believe that cash flow management cannot significantly alter the financial position of a firm, then you are grossly mistaken. But do not worry as you are in elite company. Many of the top managers too tend to make the same mistake (initially!) – to quickly learn, unlike the above case.

"Cash" is the lifeblood of any company. Hence, the efficient management of an cash flow becomes imperative for all concerns. Apart from ensuring liquidity, adept cash flow management can also play a role in the profitability of a company. In order to better manage the funds and cash, as stated at the start of the chapter companies rely on their "Cash Flow Statement". As the name says, it gives us the position and flow of the cash inside a company.

1
CHAPTER

Funds

It is a known fact that every transaction alters the position of a business. An enterprise, after every transaction, is not the same as it had been before. Thus, it can be concluded that the business is in a continuous state of change, involving an uninterrupted movement of resources into the business, within the business, and out of the business. The complexity of these flows increases with the increase in size and volume of the business. Directly or indirectly, all these flows take place through the medium of funds. So, let us first understand the meaning of the word 'Funds'.

Funds

Depending on the user's purpose, the term *funds* may be used differently.

Literally, it means a sum of money set aside, which can be drawn upon in times of need. Funds are generally created for a specific purpose. For example, your parents might set aside a specific sum in order to buy a house in future. This sum of money may be seen as a fund. A popular type of fund is a Mutual Fund, wherein a pool of money is created, with the specific purpose of investing it in the financial markets.

However, in respect of the Fund Flow Statement, the term fund indicates the 'working capital' of the business. The working capital of a business stands for the 'Current Assets' *minus* the 'Current Liabilities'. (Read the box given on page 4 to recollect these terms).

The different connotations of the term often confuse the reader. Hence, the reader will be well advised to ignore other definitions of the word for the present.

We will now discuss another important concept, with respect to the cash flow statement, i.e the *Operating Cycle.*

Bholuram: Hey Finnova! In the above definition of "funds", I find few terms that were also used in the book on *How to Read a Balance Sheet*. You know I am a *bhulakkad* (forgetful) hence, Finnova please brief me again on Current Assets, Current Liabilities and Working Capital.

Finnova: Oh! for sure, Mr. Memory Loss. On having any doubt, you can always ask me. 'Current' literally, means a flow; and in accounting, we use it in the same sense to indicate the flow through the business.

- The assets that the company looks to dispose (either by selling or by consumption) within a period of a year, are referred to as *Current Assets*. The Assets includes cash, inventory (stock), debtors, trade receivables, short-term investment of the company, etc.
- The liabilities of the company (amounts owed by the business to people who have lent money or provided goods or services on credit) that become due within a year, i.e. they need to be paid back within one year of creation of such a liability, are classified as *Current Liabilities* such as, creditors, rent payable and interest payable.
- The capital employed by a firm for conducting of its day-to-day affairs, is recorded as *Working Capital*. It is given by *Current Assets minus the Current Liabilities of the firm,* (also known as *Net Working Capital*). Gross Working Capital is the Total Current Assets of the company. So if a company has Current Assets of ₹ 200,000 and Current Liabilities of ₹ 100,000, then the Gross Working Capital of the company would be ₹ 200,000, while the net working capital or the working capital we generally talk about would be ₹ 100,000.

Operating cycle

Typical business transactions move in cycles. Cash is converted into different forms of current assets and then ultimately back to cash. The operating cycle for a particular company is the time it takes to convert these flow items back, into cash. Cash usually passes through various stages of an operating cycle during this process. Described below is a typical operating cycle for a manufacturing business.

The operating cycle starts when cash is utilized for the purchase of inventory and ends when the inventory is sold and cash is realized from the customer. In this case, the cash will pass through the stages of inventories. At last, it will get transferred through the accounts receivables and get transformed back into cash.

Fig. 1.1 ***Operating Cycle***

In the coming chapter, we shall know more about the Working Capital and in the Progress, we will be able to understand the different components that make up the operating cycle.

2

CHAPTER

Working Capital

The financial managers devote a great amount of time in the short-term financing needs of the company, negotiating favorable credit terms, controlling movement of cash, administering accounts receivable, and monitoring inventories. Managing of short-term financial needs is termed as Working Capital Management.

Working Capital

Working Capital refers to the assets held by the business with the objective of conversion to cash (including cash) during an operating cycle of the business. As illustrated in the previous chapter, the working capital (also known as *Net Working Capital* or *Net Current Assets*) is given by Current Assets *minus* the Current Liabilities of the firm. So, for instance, if a company has Current Assets of ₹ 10 million and Current Liabilities of ₹ 9 million, then the working capital of the firm would be ₹ 1 million. The working capital of a firm is the capital employed by the firm in conducting its day to day operations. The firm tries to keep its working capital at an optimum level. Higher than required working capital results in unnecessary blockage of funds, which could have resulted in extra returns if invested somewhere else. Too low working capital may result in shortage of funds in times of need.

★★★

Working Capital = Current Assets – Current Liabilities

★★★

Flow of Funds

Let us now look at the working capital of Chota Pehlwan Sweets as detailed below.

Table 2.1 ***Working Capital***

Chota Pehlwan Sweets			
Cash	₹ 200,000	Short term loans	₹ 100,000
Stock (Inventory)	₹ 200,000	Creditors (Payables)	₹ 200,000
Current Assets	**₹ 400,000**	**Current Liabilities**	**₹ 300,000**

In the above table, we can see that Chota Pehlwan Sweets must have needed some resources in order to finance, or procure the current assets of ₹ 400,000. Let us analyze as to what these possible resources could have been. The stock of ₹ 200,000, have been purchased on credit from some suppliers. That figure of ₹ 200,000 is reflected in the Current Liabilities of the company as Creditors. So, it can be said that current liabilities (creditors) has been used to finance the current assets (stock) of ₹ 200,000. Similarly, we can ascertain that the short-term loan of ₹ 100,000 has been used to finance cash balance of ₹ 100,000 (out of the total cash balance of ₹ 200,000). Hence, we have established that ₹ 300,000 out of the total Current Assets of ₹ 400,000, have been financed out of Current Liabilities. The portion of the Current Assets that have not been financed by Current Liabilities, i.e. ₹ 400,000 – ₹ 300,000 = ₹ 100,000, is what is represented as the Working Capital. This implies that some amount of resources is invested in current assets from sources of finance other than current liabilities.

Now, since it's established that the funds acted as the working capital of Chota Pehlwan Sweets Ltd., therefore, it means that any change in the position of it (funds), will only take place when there is a movement in the current assets or the current liabilities of the firm. For example, if land is purchased out of a long-term loan, there is no flow of funds. This is because land is a non-current asset, and the loan is a non-current liability. These types of transactions neither affect the current liability, nor the current assets. Hence, there is no movement in the working capital position due to the given transaction. In the same example, if the purchase is made by using a short-term loan, it would result in an increase of current liability, without an equal and corresponding increase in current asset, hence decrease the working capital, or in other words, there would be an outflow of funds.

To sum it up, *fund flow* refers to the changes in the current assets and current liabilities. If there is an increase in the working capital of the firm, we say that there has been an inflow of funds. On the other hand, if there is a decrease in the working capital of the firm, then we say that there has been an outflow of funds. This movement is vital for understanding and managing the operations of a business.

Need for Working Capital

Since, the emphasis of this book is more on the practical rather than theoretical aspects of business, we herein present a detailed illustration, explaining the workings of a business and try to illustrate how and why working capital is needed for a business.

Example 1: Ramsons

Ramson is a small retail outlet dealing in domestic appliances and entertainment electronics equipment, which has just been started by Ram.

- His investment in the showroom, display counters, furniture and fixtures and so on, was ₹ 6,000,000.
- Ram also decided to follow the straight-line method[2] of depreciation for the fixed assets, at the rate of 10 percent per annum.
- Ramsons' estimated sales were ₹ 1,500,000 per month. Out of which ₹ 500,000 would be cash sales, and ₹ 1,000,000, on credit, to be collected in four equal monthly installments, with the first installment collected at the time of sale.
- All sales would be made on a 25 percent margin on the selling price. In other words, if selling price of a merchandise item is ₹ 100 then its cost of sales would be ₹ 75.
- Supply and sales constraints would warrant carrying three months sales requirement in the form of inventory. Similarly, a month's cash expense requirements had to be held in cash balance.
- Subsequent purchases would receive a month's credit from suppliers.
- The average monthly cash requirement for meeting operating expenses other than payment for purchases amounted to ₹ 260,000.
- Ram needed to withdraw ₹ 40,000 per month for his personal needs.

[2]Refer to *How to Read a Balance Sheet-Second Edition* of Finance Made Easy Series for better understanding of the above mentioned method.

In the above example, it is clear that Ramsons is coming out with some broad norms for managing the new business, leading to issues such as:

- How much working capital would Ramsons require to start operations?
- Will he need any additional funds to the working capital during the first four months?
- Or will he have surplus working capital during the first four months?

We can instinctively answer these questions by saying that Ramsons needs working capital to pay for inventory, for all the expenses and for keeping cash balance safe. We can also say that Ramsons will receive funds from operations to meet most of these requirements. But to say exactly how much, we need to approach the problem a little more critically. This could be done by working out a schedule of cash receipts and cash payments on a monthly basis. It is also possible by preparing a monthly Profit & Loss account and Balance Sheet for the business. We prepare and display all the four of them in the next few pages.

Table 2.2 ***Schedule of Cash Payments (All figures in Rupees)***

Ramsons			
Month	**Explanation**	**Amount**	**Total**
January	Operating expenses	260,000	
	Withdrawals	40,000	
			300,000
February	January purchases	1,125,000[3]	
	Operating expenses	260,000	
	Withdrawals	40,000	
			1,425,000
March	February purchases	1,125,000	
	Operating expenses	260,000	
	Withdrawals	40,000	
			1,425,000
April	March purchases	1,125,000	
	Operating expenses	260,000	
	Withdrawals	40,000	
			1,425,000

[3]If selling price is ₹ 100, then cost of sales is ₹ 75. Therefore when monthly sales is ₹ 1,500,000, cost of sales is ₹ 1,125,000 (i.e. 75÷100×1,500,000).

Table 2.3 ***Schedule of Cash Receipts (All figures in Rupees)***

Ramsons			
Month	**Explanation**	**Amount**	**Total**
January	Cash Sales of January month	500,000	
	Credit sales of the month (first installment of January month sales)	250,000	
			750,000
February	Cash Sales of February month sales	500,000	
	Credit sales of the month (first installment of February month sales)	250,000	
	January sales (second installment of January month sales)	250,000	
			1,000,000
March	Cash Sales of March month sales)	500,000	
	Credit sales of the month (first installment of March month sales)	250,000	
	January sales (third installment of January month sales)	250,000	
	February sales (second installment of February month sales)	250,000	
			1,250,000
April	Cash Sales of April month sales	500,000	
	Credit sales of the month (first installment of April month sales)	250,000	
	January sales (fourth installment of January month sales)	250,000	
	February sales (third installment of February month sales)	250,000	
	March sales (second installment of March month sales)	250,000	
			1,500,000

We have assumed that the entire asset requirements at the first instance are financed by Ram's own capital. Working capital of Ramsons at the beginning of January was as shown in Table 2.4.

Based on the above information, we could also compute a schedule of cash receipts and payments of Ramsons for the four month, which will show the deficit or surplus of cash available to the business (as shown in Table 2.6).

Table 2.4 ***Balance Sheet as of 1st January (All figures in Rupees)***

Ramsons			
Assets	**Amount**	**Liabilities and Capital**	**Amount**
Fixed Assets	6,000,000	Capital	9,675,000[4]
Inventory	3,375,000[5]		
Cash	300,000[6]		
Total	**9,675,000**	**Total**	**9,675,000**

Table 2.5 ***Working capital of Ramsons***

Current Assets	**Amount (Rs)**
Inventory	3,375,000
Cash	300,000
Total Current Assets	3,675,000
Less: Current Liabilities	0
Working Capital	3,675,000

Table 2.6 ***Schedule of Cash Balance (All figures in Rupees)***

Ramsons				
	January	**February**	**March**	**April**
Opening Balance	300,000	750,000	325,000	150,000
Cash receipts	750,000	1,000,000	1,250,000	1,500,000
Total Cash available	1,050,000	1,750,000	1,575,000	1,650,000
Less: Cash payments	300,000	1,425,000	1,425,000	1,425,000
Cash Balance	**750,000**	**325,000**	**150,000**	**225,000**

Using the information available, we can also prepare the profit & loss account of the business for the four-month period as in Table 2.7.

Incorporating the changes in the assets, liabilities and owner(s) equity as a result of the transactions during the four months, we can also prepare the balance sheet of the business as at the end of each month.

Now, we can easily create a table containing the changes in the working capital of Ramsons and the possible sources of their funding.

[4]We are assuming that Ramsons has not taken any loans or Long Term Liability to start the enterprise. Capital has been taken as a balancing figure.

[5]Inventory has to be three months sales requirement (Refer page nos.12-13) Monthly Sales = ₹ 1,500, 000 & Cost of sales = ₹ 1,125,000. Hence, monthly inventory for three months requirement = 1,125,000 × 3 = ₹ 3,375,000.

[6]Monthly cash requirement is ₹ 300, 000.

Table 2.7 ***Profit & Loss Account for the Month Ending (All figures in Rupees)***

Ramsons				
	31-Jan	28-Feb	31-Mar	30-Apr
Total Sales	**1,500,000**	**1,500,000**	**1,500,000**	**1,500,000**
Less: Cost of Sales	1,125,000	1,125,000	1,125,000	1,125,000
Other Expenses	260,000	260,000	260,000	260,000
Depreciation[7]	50,000	50,000	50,000	50,000
Total Expenses	**1,435,000**	**1,435,000**	**1,435,000**	**1,435,000**
Net Profit[8]	65,000	65,000	65,000	65,000
Less: Drawings[9]	40,000	40,000	40,000	40,000
Retained Profits	**25,000**	**25,000**	**25,000**	**25,000**

Table 2.8 ***Schedule of Working Capital (All figures in Rupees)***

Ramsons					
Assets	**1 January**	**31 January**	**28 February**	**31 March**	**30 April**
Current assets	3,675,000	4,875,000	4,950,000	5,025,000	5,100,000
Less. Current Liabilities	0	1,125,000	1,125,000	1,125,000	1,125,000
Working Capital	**3,675,000**	**3,750,000**	**3,825,000**	**3,900,000**	**3,975,000**
Change in Working Capital	**0**	**75,000**	**75,000**	**75,000**	**75,000**
Funds from Operation (All figures in Rupees)					
Net Profit	65,000	65,000	65,000	65,000	
Add: Depreciation[10]	50,000	50,000	50,000	50,000	
Total Funds generated from operations	115,000	115,000	115,000	115,000	
Less: Withdrawals	40,000	40,000	40,000	40,000	
Net additions to Working Capital	**75,000**	**75,000**	**75,000**	**75,000**	

[7]Depreciation for the year comes to ₹ 600,000 (₹ 6,000,000 x 10%). Therefore, depreciation for the month is ₹ 50,000 (₹ 600,000÷12).

[8]Here we are ignoring Corporate Income Tax

[9]Ramsons monthly withdrawal has been considered as a dividend and not as salary.

[10]Depreciation is just an allocation of fair proportion of the depreciable amount in each accounting period during the expected useful life of the assets, it is not an actual outflow of funds, and hence we add back depreciation to arrive at the total funds generated from operations.

Table 2.9 ***Balance Sheet as at the end of Year (All figures in Rupees)***

Ramsons											
Assets	**1-Jan**	**31-Jan**	**28-Feb**	**31-Mar**	**30-Apr**	**Liabilities & Capital**	**1-Jan**	**31-Jan**	**28-Feb**	**31-Mar**	**30-Apr**
Cash	300,000	750,000	325,000	150,000	225,000	Accounts Payable	0	1,125,000	1,125,000	1,125,000	1,125,000
Receivable		750,000	1,250,000	1,500,000	1,500,000						
Inventory	3,375,000	3,375,000	3,375,000	3,375,000	3,375,000						
Current Assets	**3,675,000**	**4,875,000**	**4,950,000**	**5,025,000**	**5,100,000**	**Current Liabilities**	**0**	**1,125,000**	**1,125,000**	**1,125,000**	**1,125,000**
Fixed Assets	6,000,000	6,000,000	6,000,000	6,000,000	6,000,000	Capital	9,675,000	9,675,000	9,675,000	9,675,000	9,675,000
Less: Depreciation		50,000	100,000	150,000	200,000	Add: Retained earnings		25,000	50,000	75,000	100,000
Net Fixed Assets	**6,000,000**	**5,950,000**	**5,900,000**	**5,850,000**	**5,800,000**	**Owners' Equity**	**9,675,000**	**9,700,000**	**9,725,000**	**9,750,000**	**9,775,000**
Total Assets	**9,675,000**	**10,825,000**	**10,850,000**	**10,875,000**	**10,900,000**	**Total Liabilities & Capital**	**9,675,000**	**10,825,000**	**10,850,000**	**10,875,000**	**10,900,000**

Reconciling Increase in Working Capital

In the above example, we were following the changes in the working capital, and we noticed that these changes were due to only funds generated by operations. It is easy for us to track the changes in the working capital over the periods, starting with - the beginning of the business and ending with the close during the month of April.

Table 2.10 ***Working Capital Requirement (All figures in Rupees)***

Ramsons	
Working capital as on January 1	3,675,000
Add: additions during the January	75,000
Working capital as on February 1	3,750,000
Add: additions during the February	75,000
Working capital as on March 1	3,825,000
Add: additions during the March	75,000
Working capital as on April 1	3,900,000
Add: additions during the April	75,000
Working capital as on May 1	3,975,000

In this chapter we have seen how the fund flows. In the next segment, we will discuss the need for investment in fixed assets and current assets.

3 CHAPTER

Capital Invested in Business

In the Ramsons example, we saw that Ramsons kept reinvesting the extra funds generated back into the business. And as the money ploughed back, Ramsons generated profits. Often, this ploughing back of profits is known as *retained earnings*. Where has Ramsons invested the money? It is easy to answer this question too, because the balance sheet of the business shows us what Ramsons has done with the money to start with. Refer to the first balance sheet and you will find that Ramsons had fixed assets, shop room and facilities, inventory, goods or merchandise purchased for resale, and some cash for meeting expenses and personal needs. In the later balance sheet, we observe that the current assets of the company are increasing progressively. So, Ramsons invested its money in increasing its working capital. We review these current assets items, and progressively enhance our understanding.

Need to Invest in Cash

It is difficult to perceive cash kept in a vault as an investment. Rather, you would be thinking how can cash itself be an investment? But you will realize that a certain (minimum) amount of cash is necessary for any business. Take a simple case: if you are a retailer, will you probably send a customer away, who does not have the exact change? You can only entertain him if you keep the change. The change you keep is your investment in cash. Similarly, you will have to pay your employees and suppliers on a specific time. In order to do that, you need to keep some cash. This amount or cash will help you meet the day-to-day requirements. The amount is determined after taking into account the regularity, and the cash inflow and outflow and also the uncertainties related to these. Obviously, as your business grows, the need for cash will also grow. The need for cash will also be influenced by your *need* for investment in other assets.

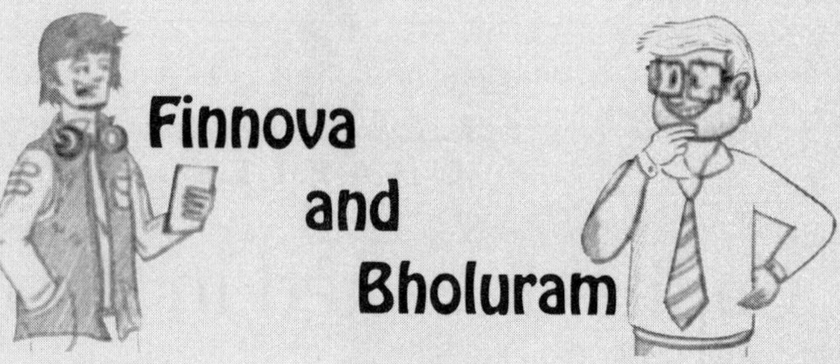

Finnova: Bhola, we often see that a company that has some good amount of liquid cash has the ability to quickly handle an unexpected financial situation, like paying the salary to its employees, paying off its suppliers, for paying back short-term debts. Liquid cash also comes in use when a company suddenly plans for an investment for better returns in future.

Not only that, when a company suddenly falls into a loop of economic and legal crisis, it needs cash in hand for speedy legal services.

Cash reserves may need to be drawn when a company's sales do not meet the expected levels or that prices will have to be lowered unexpectedly to match a peer competitor.

But, tell me in case there is excess of liquid cash with the company what will it result in?

Bholuram: In such a case, from an investor's point of view, I would notice that the company is too short-sighted for not taking care of the future returns through best possible investments.

Another thing to notice would be that the company would possibly have sold its fixed assets to hike the cash in hand for using all the liquid cash in paying off its other priorities, such as high technology usage in the packaging of final products.

Finnova: What if the company has run into a negative cash crisis or comes down to zero?

Bholuram: A company that spends more cash on purchases than they earn on sales can end up with a zero or negative cash in hand. This would mean that the company would become unable to pay for debts or loans and other ongoing expenses. This may eventually cause business failure, but without losing hope, better business strategies can be to increase the cash or cash inflow.

Finnova: Hmm, not bad ☺

Need to Invest in Receivables

In most business situations, it's necessary to grant credit to customers. This could be either because of competition, or because of the custom of trade.

When granting a credit, (a good), or a service is provided to the customer, and instead of immediately paying cash, the customer promises to pay it at a later date. For example, a large portion of Ramsons sales are due to the credit (installments) they are offering. This amount represents an asset for the business, as this is the amount that it owns from the customer, who now becomes its debtor. This amount is shown in the Balance Sheet as accounts receivable (also commonly known as debtors or sundry debtors). The opportunity aspect of this credit granted is that, you are deferring the receipt of cash to the extent of the receivables amount.

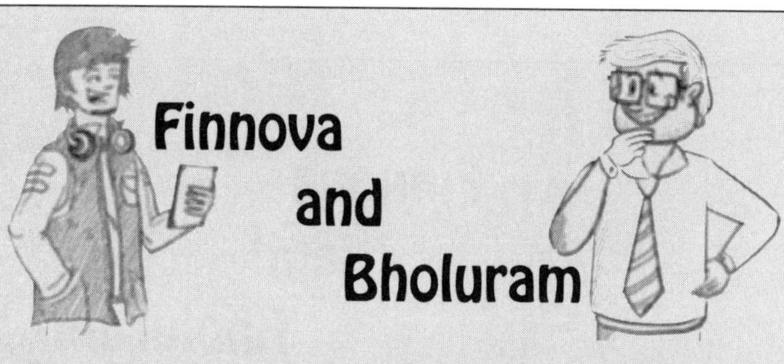

Finnova: Tell me Bhola, what happens when a firm faces a zero receivables problem?

Bholuram: Well I think if accounts receivables go down to zero, then a firm is getting back the future earnings very quick (in short span) in the form of cash and as such, it increases the company's working capital (defined as current assets minus current liabilities).

Finnova: And what happens when accounts receivables increases?

Bholuram: When accounts receivable goes up, this is considered as use of cash on the company's cash flow statement because the company is increasing the time it takes to receive money owed by others to it.

Finnova: Hmmm..ok ☺

Need to Invest in Inventory

You can appreciate the need for carrying inventory. In order to carry on operations unhindered, we need to have a sufficient amount of merchandise on hand. The availability and regularity of supply, the frequency of client orders and so on, will determine the quantum we have to keep in store. All the same, we should carry some inventory in most cases. Inventory is also held, whenever there is a time lag between procurement, and use of inventory of materials & supplies like in manufacturing enterprises – thus, manufacturing firms tend to have four types of inventories i.e., raw materials, work-in-progress, finished goods and stocks-&-spares inventories.

Related scenario is in the case with non-merchandise inventory, such as office and factory supplies. We have to carry a minimum stock of these items to ensure smooth operations. We also know that there are several expenses that are to be paid before we actually use the services, such as rent, insurance and so on. In other words, we invest our money in these items of assets in order to ensure smooth operations.

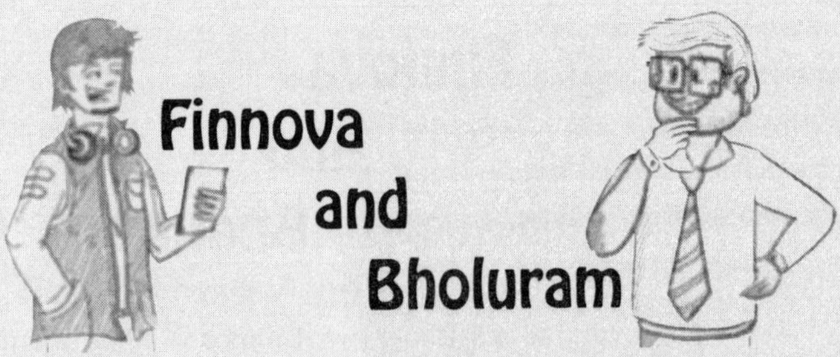

Finnova: What if a company faces a situation of zero inventory?

Bholuram: That would mean a stock-out situation for the company. Customers buy inventory from stores and low inventory or reduction in inventory may mean that the sales are going to be low and hence, would affect the store's total revenue.

When finished goods come less in the market it means that the resources are kept idle or there is not enough raw material coming into the firm to produce finished goods. This could mean that the firm is incapable of buying raw materials now due to fewer current assets.

Finnova: Ok. Agreed.

Need to Invest in Fixed (Non-Current) Assets

We have seen the importance of current assets. They are very important for operating the business. Now, the necessity for having adequate fixed facilities to conduct the business is clear. The amount we have invested, in our example of Ramsons, for the shop, furniture and fixtures, are for creating the facilities required for carrying on the business. As the business expands, it may be required to extend the fixed capacity of the business. For example, suppose a bottling plant has set up a machine that can produce 100,000 bottles per week. With an expanding business, a need may be felt to increase the capacity to 200,000 bottles per week. In such a case, the management will have to invest additional resources to procure the extra machines to set up additional capacity.

It is also necessary for us to understand that the need for fixed asset investments and current asset investments will vary from business to business. A trading company may require very little investment in fixed assets and a very large investment in current assets. A capital intensive manufacturing unit may need large investments in factory, technology and equipment. Fixed Asset requirements are also known as *jump investments* as they are determined by specific firms at given levels of their volumes of activities.

Determining the Working Capital Requirement

Understanding the existing capital needs, and how are they financed, will help us in comprehending the process of financing of the business, and the flows of funds within the business. The first question we have to answer is how much working capital is needed to start the operations. We could determine the amount of working capital required and compare the same with the existing (estimated) working capital to see, whether it is sufficient or whether there is any excess available.[11]

Let's again look at the Ramsons example.

Operating requirements of the business:

1. One month's cash expenses, other than payment to creditors, to be kept in cash.
   - A minimum of ₹ 300,000 of average cash on hand.
2. Keep three months' sales requirement in inventory.
   - During the first month, they start with three months' sales worth of inventory.
   - Sale per month is ₹ 1,500,000.

[11]Please note that there are more complex tools used by professionals to determine the capital requirements but they are beyond the scope of this book.

- Sold at a gross margin of 25 percent on sales.
- Therefore, inventory required to be maintained is three times 75 percent of the monthly sales.
- ₹ 1,500,000 × 0.75 × 3 = ₹ 3,375,000.

3. Every month, one-third of the sales are made on cash, and two-third of the sales are on credit.
4. The credit sales are to be collected in four installments.
   - Cash collection during the month will be cash sales.
   - One-fourth of the credit sales of the period and one-fourth of three previous months will be taken as credit sales (being monthly installments received from customer).
5. During the first month, we will collect from sales for cash, ₹ 500,000, and from the first installment of 25 percent of the credit sales:

Table 3.1 ***First Month Sales and Cash Collections (All figures in Rupees)***

Ramsons		
	Details	**Amount**
Cash Sales	500,000	
Credit Sales	1,000,000	
Total Sales		1,500,000
Cash Sales	500,000	
First installment in cash	250,000	
Total Cash Collection		**750,000**

Credit period allowed on the sales will be as follows:

Total amount of credit granted on one month's sales, is the total sales of the month, less the first installment to be paid by the buyer. This means, Ramsons effectively makes credit sales of ₹ 750,000 per month. This ₹ 750,000 will be collected in three equal monthly installments.

Table 3.2

Particulars/ Installment	**Amount**		**1st**		**2nd**		**3rd**		**4th**
Cash Sale	500,000								
Credit Sale	1,000,000	→	(250,000) =	→	(250,000) =	→	(250,000) =	→	(250,000) =
Due			750,000		500,000		250,000		0

This will mean:

- From the date of sale, till the payment of the second installment, ₹ 750,000 is due for one month. A credit of ₹ 750,000 is granted for one month.
- From the date of the second installment, till the payment of the third installment, ₹ 500,000 is due for one month. A credit of ₹ 500,000 is granted for two months.
- From the date of the third installment, till the payment of the fourth installment, ₹ 250,000 is due for one month. A credit of ₹ 250,000 is granted for three months.

Therefore, we could summarize Ramsons need for funds for current asset financing to start operations at the beginning of the period, as follows:

During the first month, Ramsons will make one-third of the total sales generating ₹ 500,000, in cash. The remaining two third of the sales will be on installment credit, where ₹ 250,000 will be collected in cash and ₹ 750,000 will be collected in three further installments. Thus, we need some additional funds to finance our granting credit to the customers.

Table 3.3[12]

3 months inventory	₹ 3,375,000
One month expenses as cash	₹ 300,000
Total	**₹ 3,675,000**

Similarly, we would need to replenish the inventory and make payments for the expenses. We shall examine these with the help of the balance sheet and profit & loss account of Ramsons, for the first four months.

Future Capital Requirements

Any business including Ramsons would require additional capital for two purposes:

- Financing additional non-current assets; and
- Financing additional working capital.

Investment in fixed assets is required to expand the capacity, or to improve the current facilities for operation. Usually, additions to investments

[12]Follow point 2 under *Determining the Working Capital Requirement* section in this chapter for better understanding.

are judged on the basis of their ability to reduce the present costs, or to increase the present output (sales).

If Ramsons invests in another shop, or in an expansion of the existing shop, it will require funds for an investment in the fixed assets, and also for increasing the current assets. We also notice that whenever an additional investment is to be made in non-current assets, we have to use the funds (working capital) available. Similarly, when our non-current assets are sold, the sale provides funds, or results in a source of funds.

Additional working capital is required to finance an increased holding of inventory, increased credit to customers and increased cash holding requirement (see Table 3.4).

Let us try to review the five-period balance sheet of Ramsons in table 3.4, in page no. 23, to see the changes and evaluate the working capital situation. We can achieve this by, first, finding out the changes in each item over the previous period.

The changes in the fixed assets are represented by the accumulated depreciation only. There were no additions to fixed assets during the period. Reduction in the fixed assets due to depreciation is a non-cash transaction.

On the liability side also, there was no transaction involving long-term liabilities or capital. The only change in the long-term items is the increase in the retained earnings.

Thus, all the changes are in the area of the working capital. The net change in the working capital, as we have seen earlier, is an increase of ₹ 75,000 per period. How did this come about? This leads us to the changes in the current assets and current liabilities. There was no change in the inventory during the period. The only items which experienced change are cash and receivables. The current liability saw changes in the accounts payable in the first period. The increase in the receivables needed funds to finance it, and this was provided in parts by the increase in payables, thereby having not much impact on the working capital. Whenever an increase in the current assets is offset by an equal increase in the current liabilities, the net impact on the funds required for working capital is zero.

This means that the only other item that could have financed the change in working capital would be the funds generated by operations.

The operations provided a net profit of ₹ 65,000 during each period. We have made an expiration of fixed assets in the amount of ₹ 50,000 per month. Depreciation is a non-fund transaction, meaning, no cash goes away from the entity, and hence, the fund provided by operations will include that too. Thus, operations generated ₹ 115,000 per period. The owner

Table 3.4 *Change in Balance Sheet[13] over the Previous Period as at the end of Month (All figures in Rupees)*

Ramsons									
Assets	**31 Jan**	**28 Feb**	**31 Mar**	**30 Apr**	**Liabilities & Capital**	**31 Jan**	**28 Feb**	**31 Mar**	**30 Apr**
Cash	450,000	-425,000	-175,000	75,000	Accounts Payable	1,125,000	0	0	0
Receivable	750,000	500,000	250,000	0					
Inventory	0	0	0	0					
Current assets	1,200,000	75,000	75,000	75,000	Current Liabilities	1,125,000	0	0	0
Fixed Assets	0	0	0		Capital	0	0	0	0
Less: Depreciation[14]	50,000	50,000	50,000	50,000	Add: Retained Earnings	25,000	25,000	25,000	25,000
Net fixed assets	-50,000	-50,000	-50,000	-50,000	Owners Equity	25,000	25,000	25,000	25,000
Net Change in Assets side	1,150,000	25,000	25,000	25,000	Net Change in Liabilities & Capital side	1,150,000	25,000	25,000	25,000

[13]Refer Chapter 2, Table 2.8 and Table 2.9

[14]Depreciation is a non-cash transaction as it is just an allocation of fair proportion of the depreciable amount in each accounting period during the expected useful life of the assets.

regularly withdrew cash of ₹ 40,000 per period, leaving in the business, additional resources of ₹ 75,000 per period, which is the change in the working capital.

Table 3.5

	1 January	31 January	28 February	31 March	30 April
Working Capital	3,675,000	3,750,000	3,825,000	3,900,000	3,975,000

Thus in the above example, we have seen how the funds from operations, provided an additional working capital to finance a required cash holding. Hence, the source for additional working capital was the funds from operations, and the cash withdrawal, were the application of funds.

We can summarize the normal uses of funds (working capital) as follows:

1. Acquisition of new non-current assets (fixed assets or intangible assets like technology license);
2. Repayment of non-current debt (say, long-term loans);
3. Profit distribution to owners (popularly, known as dividends paid);
4. Increase in the balance of working capital (current assets - current liabilities).

The figure shown below is shown to mark out the same in an easier way.

If the operations are unsuccessful, they may use funds (and even need more funds) rather than provide funds. The following are included within the application of funds as used in the fund flow statement.

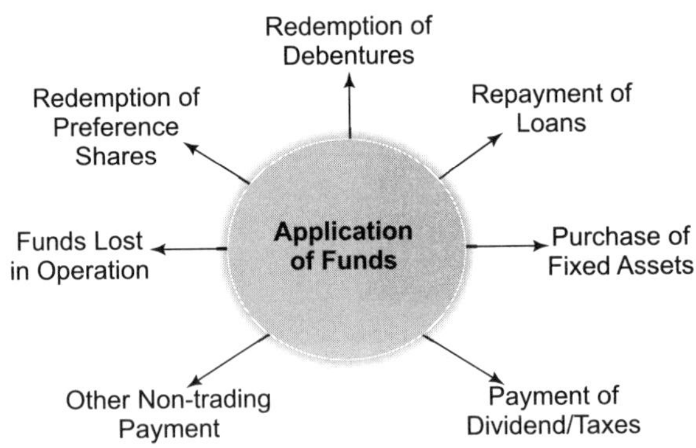

Fig. 3.1 ***Various Applications of Funds***

Possible Sources of Working Capital

We have seen that working capital is required to finance that portion of current assets, which are not financed by current liabilities. We also studied that the investments represented by current assets are converted into cash during the operating cycle. Under normal circumstances, every unit of investment in working capital is converted to cash at the end of the cycle.

When we are looking at the possible sources of working capital, the most important source represents 'internal generations'. The very idea of internal sources implies that there is something 'external' as well.

The figure below shows various sources of Working Capital.

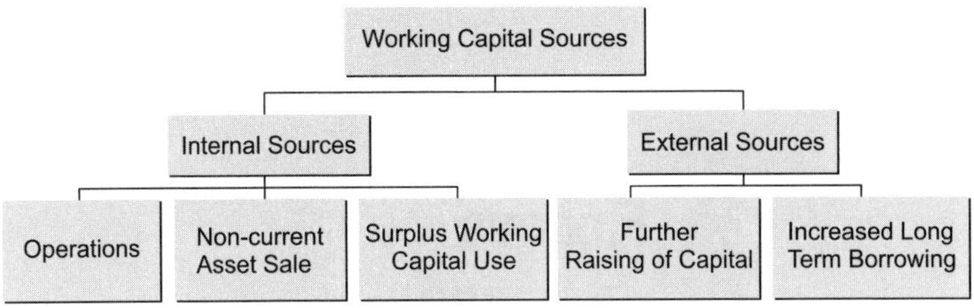

Fig. 3.1 ***Sources of Working Capital***

Internal Sources

When we are looking for sources of funds, it is natural to start from home. What do we have? While examining the need for working capital, we could also make an assessment as to whether the existing working capital is sufficient or not. Thus, the first internal source is any excess working capital asset i.e., any existing current assets that might be put to better use. For example, if a company has a short-term investment in marketable securities (like highly liquid mutual funds, or government securities) then the firm could liquidate the same, and put these funds to spruce up its working capital management.

The second internal source is disposal of any non-current assets. If we have any non-current assets, which do not have any use, they could be disposed of, thereby generating funds for additional working capital. This, however, is not a regular and continuing source of funds, as there would be a limit to the amount of non-current assets that can be disposed off.

We have seen earlier that every profitable sale brings with it, funds in excess of what was expended on the goods sold. In other words, a profit generated by the business contributes towards additional working capital. But that figure may be slightly undervalued. This is because whenever we record a profit generating revenue item, we deduct all the expenses, which have been incurred to earn the revenue, so that we gain profit at the end of the day. Now, there may be a few items which though were counted as expense (example depreciation), but did not involve any real outflow of funds. Hence, the profit measured does not reflect the actual amount of funds available.

Therefore, in order to assess the actual fund generated from current operations, we must add with profits, all those items of 'expense' not involving the use of funds, during the current period. One common example of such an item is depreciation. Another example is amortization expense for the year.

Bholuram: Hey Finnova, I recall coming across the terms Amortization and Depreciation in our earlier book *How to Read a Balance Sheet-Second edition.* Can I say that you are depreciating my brains by cramming with financial jargons?

Finnova: No Bholu!! It will be amortization. Let me recapture the definitions of amortization and depreciation for you:

- Valuation of the fixed assets is usually made on the basis of their original cost. However, since the assets have a limited life, the cost will expire along with the expiration of the life. Thus, the valuation of the asset is reduced in proportion to the expired life of the asset. Such expired cost is referred to as 'depreciation' in accounting.
- Many intangible assets have a limited life too. Examples are patent rights, franchise rights and so on. Since they have a limited useful life, the cost of acquiring such assets has to be transformed into expired costs over such useful life. This process of expiration of the cost of an intangible asset is called 'amortization'.

In reality, the material effect of amortization and depreciation is almost the same.

In your case, since I consider your brain as an intangible asset (albeit, minute) hence, I will call it amortization than depreciation.

External Sources

External sources of funds are resources raised from outside the organization to augment funds availability for any of the uses discussed earlier. Normally, there are only two ways of doing the same:

1. By the owners contributing additional capital, that is, by raising more capital through a medium like issue of new equity shares.
2. By increasing long-term borrowings, for example, by taking long-term loans from a bank or through issue of debentures/bonds.

Short-term creditors are not included as a source of working capital since we have already defined working capital as 'Current Assets minus Current Liabilities' above. Working capital, therefore, represents long-term investments in current assets and hence, short-term borrowings will not increase the working capital – rather, it'll be part of & affecting the working capital amounts.

In Table 3.6 shown below is the list sources of funds, in the way they are usually presented in the funds flow or working capital.

Let us move to the next chapter discussing factors affecting Fund Flow in an organization.

Table 3.6

Sources of Funds
Additional long term borrowing
Funds from Operations[15]
New issue of share capital
New issue of debentures/bonds
Sale of long term investments (another non-current assets like fixed assets)
Sale proceeds of fixed assets
Dividends (or withdrawals by owners.)
Increase in working capital
Purchase of long term investment
Redemption of debentures/bonds
Repayment of long term loans
Redemption of redeemable preference share capital

[15]Funds from Operations, as we have already seen, consist of the net profit for the year, as increased by the non-cash, non-operating expenses, and reduced by non-cash, non-operating incomes. It will be discussed in greater details later

4

CHAPTER

Factors Affecting Fund Requirements

From the discussions we have had earlier, it is not difficult to fathom that there are innumerable factors affecting the fund or net working capital requirements. Herein, we discuss some of them:

- **Nature and type of business:** A firm that provides brokerage services may require less working capital than a firm, which carries on a business of merchandising. The merchandising firm would require working capital to carry inventory, give credit and so on. Similarly, a manufacturing firm may require more working capital than a retailer. The manufacturing company will have to carry inventory of raw materials, work-in-progress and finished goods.
- **Sales Volume:** Working capital requirements are directly influenced by the sales volume. With growth in the sales volume, we need to carry more inventories, increase the volume of customer's receivables, and also the operating expenses. It is possible that all the expenses do not move up proportionally, however, some of these increases need to be financed. It is also possible that granting extended credits could bring about an increase in the sales volume. In other words, by investing more funds, we could increase the volume of sales.
- **Seasonality of Operations:** Fund requirements for the business may be seasonal. Say for example, in industries using agricultural raw materials (such as Turmeric and Groundnut), it would be more advantageous during the harvest season. The materials that are required for year round production might be procured during a few months. In case of consumer retailing (such as a television manufacturer), it may be necessary to hold large inventories during a festive season. Most of the fund requirements are restricted to a limited

period, and if we provide funds on a permanent basis, then we may have idle funds during most part of the year.

- **Length of the Operating Cycle:** Yet another important aspect, which may condition the fund requirement, is the velocity of circulation of the current assets. In other words, the length of the operating cycle will influence the need for funds. The shorter is the duration of an operating cycle, faster will be the conversion of money invested in current assets into cash and hence, lesser would be the need for the net working capital. So, heavy engineering firms and construction giants need to plan their working capital over a long period given their long operating cycles.
- **Suppliers:** The net working capital fund requirement is also influenced by the terms of the suppliers. The credit terms extended by the suppliers will determine the amount of additional funds required.

★★★

A firm, which carries a month's inventory and grants only a month's credit to its customers, will need to fund the inventory cost of two months' sales. If it could avail two months' credit from the suppliers, the need for funding inventory and receivables will be nil.

★★★

Finnova: I have some work for you Bholu. You have to match the following firms exactly with the features that have affected their working capital in the table given below.

Soilbuild Construction Group Ltd	Its retail *sales volume* went down in 2015-16
Coca Cola	Its *nature and type of business* generates more working capital for carrying inventory.

Shoppers' Stop	Its *seasonality of operations* affects its working capital generation.
Colgate	It needs to plan the need for funds as per the length of its operating cycle

Bholuram: Let me try… It should be in this order:

Shoppers' Stop	Its retail *sales volume* went down in 2015-16
Colgate	Its *nature and type of business* generates more working capital for carrying inventory.
Coca Cola	Its *seasonality of operations* affects its working capital generation.
Soilbuild Construction Group Ltd	It needs to plan the need for funds as per the length of its operating cycle

Finnova: Wow!!!! Bhola you nailed all of them ☺

The following illustration should help our discussion even further:

Example 1: Ranbir Ltd

Ranbir Ltd. is a small firm engaged in the trade of plastic bottles. The firm carries an average balance of ₹ 100,000 of accounts payable, payable in 30 days, and an average accounts receivable of ₹ 150,000, receivable in 45 days. What would be the working capital requirements of the firm?

Solution:

Assuming continuous flow of business to the firm, it will have to keep a net working capital for the differences of the receipts from customers and fund required for meeting the payables. The computation in such a case will be as follows:

Table 4.1

Fund required to meet payable due within 30 days	₹ 100,000
Less: Funds received from customers within 30 days: Received in 45 days, that is, ₹ 150,000 × 30/45	₹ 100,000
Fund required in the form of additional net working capital	NIL

Hence, the firm would need no new working capital. Now, if we assume the time taken for the collection of receivables as 90 days, the situation will be:

Table 4.2

Fund required to meet payable due within 30 days	₹ 100,000
Less: Funds received from customers within 30 days: Received in 45 days, that is, ₹ 150,000 × 30/90	₹ 50,000
Fund required in the form of additional net working capital	₹ 50,000

We could summarize the discussion we had, with respect to the need for working capital by saying that the ability of the firm to circulate cash in its operating cycle is the vital and important factor in determining the amount of working capital required.

Bholuram: I have a quick query here Finnova... can you tell me how do the huge retail stores such as Walmart, Big Bazar, Shoppers Stop and so on control their working capital...??

Finnova: Bhola, such retail departmental store chains typically have very strong Working Capital control policies, wherein they will purchase goods on credit from the vendors (say, Dabur or HUL or Peter England or Videocon...) and they would be sold at a lower price than the MRP to the customer on an on-time cash payment basis (be it directly through cash or indirectly via debit/credit card)... thus, there is a zero accounts receivable situation.

On the other hand, each firm these stores have a deal with, give them a considerable amount of time to pay it back, considering the total percentage of sale on the whole stock taken from that firm within a particular duration of time. In such cases, there is a lot of cash going out as interest along with the original amount for paying back which continues after each interval making space for a high accounts payable on the balance sheet.

Bholuram: Oh! I see...

In other words, the firm tries to circulate its cash as fast as possible through the following cycle:

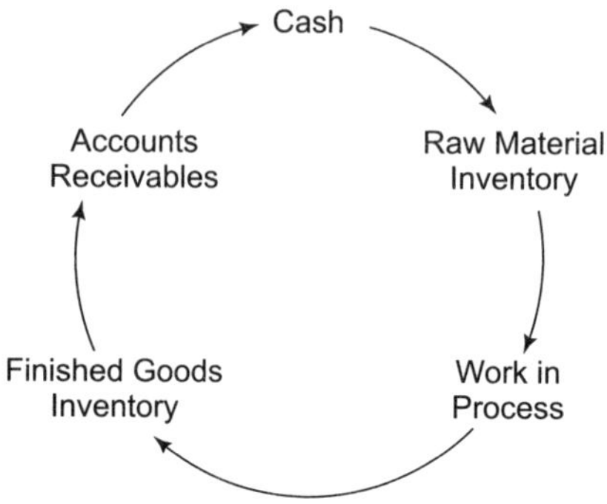

Fig. 4.1 ***Cash Flow Cycle***

Bholuram: Hey Finnova, I had once heard about the cash conversion cycle. Still curious to know, I seek your guidance.

Finnova: The Cash Conversion Cycle includes the number of days a company requires to convert resources (like raw materials or unfinished goods) into cash flows by selling the finished products. This cycle includes calculation of the time period during which every cash input into the business is committed only into the production and sales processes before it is converted into cash through the accounts receivable process.

The cash conversion process gives insight into the financial stability of a company because it reflects the time period during which all the available current assets are used for business processes and therefore cannot be available to make investments for gaining greater returns. Hence, shorter cash conversion cycle does not affect the financial stability of the company as less assets are used during the production and sale process.

Bholuram: How is it different from Operating Cycle?

Finnova: As I mentioned earlier, the Cash Conversion Cycle basically represents the actual cash position of a company by equating the cash flowing in and the cash flowing out while buying inventory (raw material purchase means cash going out), selling inventory (sales means cash coming in), collecting cash from customers (accounts receivable) and actually paying your suppliers (accounts payable). Whereas, the Operating Cycle assumes that you have paid the supplier at the time of purchases and neglects the credit period that suppliers provide their customers. (no time taken for accounts payable).

Bholuram: I bring up such great questions, isn't it?

Finnova: You bet J

However, the exact amount needed to be invested in all these will be determined by the period and quantum of the holding of each of these elements. This, in turn, is also influenced by the factors we discussed in this section such as the type and pace of business, etc.

5

CHAPTER

Fund Flow Statement

A Fund Flow Statement is also known as a '*Statement of Sources and Application of Funds*' or '*How Came and Where Gone Statement*'. The term "*flow*" implies a continuous movement, or circulation. It's a major change in a particular component during an accounting period. It is the flow of the funds, which results in changes of the financial statements from the preceding accounting period. This can easily be depicted using a picture.

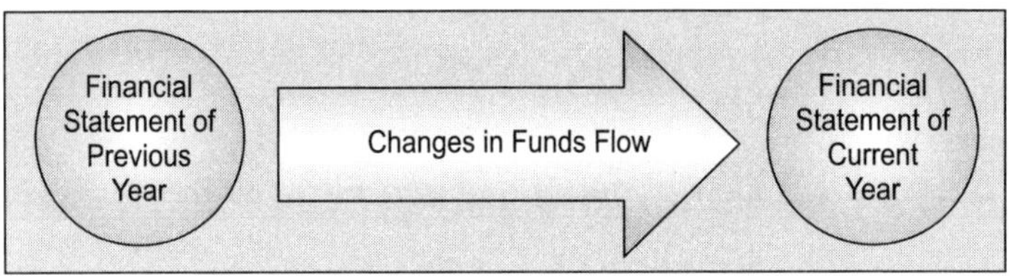

Fig. 5.1 ***Changes in Fund Flow***

The Funds Flow Equations

The Fund Flow Statement is based on the following equation:

Sources of Funds – Applications of Funds = Change in Working Capital

The above equation clarifies a well-known fact. It says that the difference between the sources and application of funds in a business, will determine the change in working capital of a firm. If sources of funds are greater than the application of funds, then we would have an increase in the working capital of the firm, whereas, if the application of funds is more than the sources of funds, then there would be a decrease in the working capital of the firm.

The Format

To prepare a Fund Flow Statement, we will have to compute funds from operation and also create a statement of changes in the working capital. The following figures give you an idea of the components of a Fund Flow Statement.

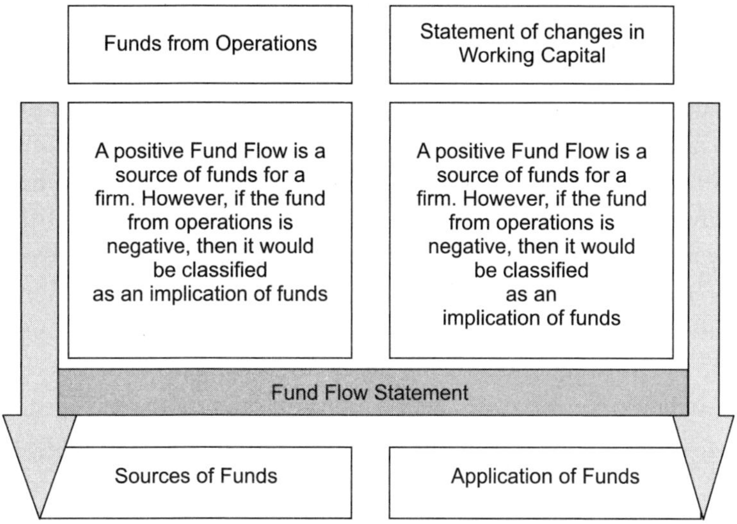

Fig. 5.2 ***Components of Fund Flow Statement***

Funds Flow from Operations

Funds from operations, also known as trading profits or trading income, are an important source of fund, especially for established firms. 'Profit' here, would mean the excess of revenue over all other expenses. This profit is there irrespective of the fact that the sale was a *cash sale* or a *credit sale*. If an item of ₹ 500 is sold for cash for ₹ 750, there is a profit of ₹ 250. This transaction here consists of two elements, i.e.:

a) Reduction of stock by ₹ 500 (working capital/flow item)

b) Increase in profit by ₹ 250 (non-current item).

Here, we receive cash ₹ 750. Up to ₹ 500, the reduction in one current asset (stock) will be balanced via an increase in the other item (cash), hence keeping the working capital unchanged for that portion. However, with the extra ₹ 250 cash earned, the working capital would increase. This ₹ 250 profit is nothing but the funds from operations of the particular firm.

However, there are certain items, which though classified as expenses, do not incur any real outflow of funds. They are mere accounting entries in the books of accounts, which though reduce the profits but do not involve any funds outlay. An often sighted example would be that of depreciation or amortization. While we do make adjustments for depreciation in our books, there is no actual payment that a business makes as a result of depreciation. So, the logical thing would be adding back the depreciation figure to the profits' of the company to find out the actual increase in funds on account of fund flow from operations.

Simultaneously, all those incomes and expenses, which do not form part of the normal operations of the business, need to be adjusted. So, all such items, such as profit/loss arising out of sales of fixed assets, income arising out of investments need to be adjusted for. We will subtract all the non-operational income that has been considered, when calculating the profits of the company. Similarly, we will add all the expenses that are of a non-operational nature to the profits of the company to get the funds from operations. Therefore the final figure obtained after adding non-cash expenses, subtracting non-operational income, and adding non-operational expenses, to the profits of the company, is that which is known as the funds from operations.

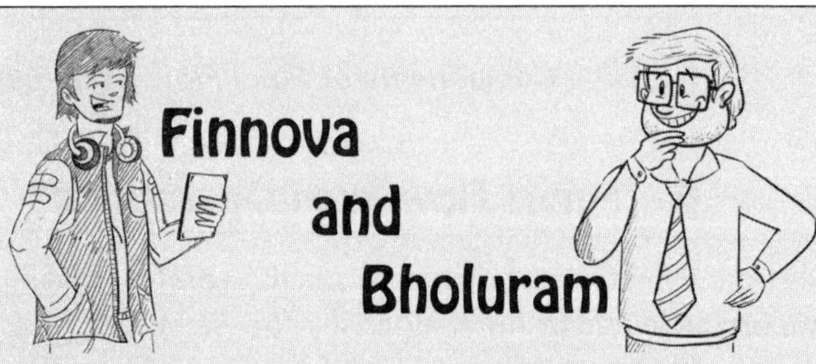

Bholuram: Hey Finnova. You are complicating things. You said "the normal operations of the Business…".What do you mean by the normal operations of the Company?

Finnova: Look Bholu, a firm is normally set up to perform a particular business activity. It regularly performs that activity and derives profit by the virtue of performing that activity. Such operations, forming the core of the business are known as normal operations and such income, derived from the main-line of the business is known as operating income/ operating profit. Apart from this core activity, a firm may also end up deriving profit from certain other non-core activities of the business. These activities fall outside the purview of the normal operations of the business and any income derived from these are known as non-operating income. To give you an example, a grocery store may derive some income, both from selling vegetables and from the interest that it earns as a result of it having a bank saving account. Here, income derived from selling of vegetables is classified as operating income, while interest income earned is a non-operating income.

Bholuram: So, I can say that currently Finnova is doing an abnormal operation!

Finnova: Shut up. Don't confuse others (as well as yourself).

Example 3: Karan Arjun

Table 5.1 ***Profit and Loss Account for the year ended December 31, 2016 (All figures in Rupees Millions)***

Karan Arjun Limited		
Particulars	**Details**	**Amount**
Sales net		350.00
Other income*		10.00
Total Revenue		**360.00**
Less: Cost of goods sold		150.00
Gross profit		**210.00**
Less: operating expenses		
Personnel	60.00	
Depreciation & amortization	11.90	
Other expenses	13.10	85.00
Operating profit		**125.00**
Less: Interest		15.00
Profit before taxes		**110.00**
Less: Income tax provision		55.00
Net profit after tax		**55.00**
Less: Dividends		20.00
Net Profit Retained		**35.00**

**Other income includes ₹ 1 million profits on sale of furniture.*

Note: *Furniture and fixtures costing ₹ 2 million, with accumulated depreciation of ₹ 1 million, were sold for cash at ₹ 2 million.*

Based on the discussion we had, the fund flow statement would show funds from operations of Karan Arjun Ltd. as follows:

Table 5.2 ***Fund from Operations for the year ended December 31, 2016 (All figures in Rupees Millions)***

Karan Arjun Limited		
Particular	**Details**	**Amount**
Operations:		
Net income	55.00	
Add: depreciation & amortization	11.90	**66.90**
Less: Profit on Sale of furniture		1.00
Total funds provided from operations		**65.90**

Hence, we observe that the funds from operations are equal to the net profit for the period increased by the non-cash and non-business expenses that were taken into consideration which creating the profit & loss statement (for example depreciation, expenses written off, and loss on sale of fixed assets) and reduced by non-cash non-business income taken in the profit & loss account (for example profit on sale of fixed assets, investments, profit from revaluation of fixed assets, and other non-operating incomes).

Example 4: M/s Johnny Lever and sons

From the following profit & loss account of M/s Johnny Lever and Sons, calculate the amount of funds from operation.

Table 5.3 ***Profit and Loss Account for the year ending 31st March 2016 (All figures in Rupees)***

M/s Johnny Lever and Sons			
Particulars	**Amount**	**Particulars**	**Amount**
To Salary	100,000	By Gross Profit	1,500,000
To Depreciation	250,000	By Profit on sale of Plant	500,000
To Loss on sale of Machinery	500,000	By Interest	400,000
To Office Expenses	400,000	By Dividend	100,000
To Net Profit	1,250,000		
Total	**2,500,000**		**2,500,000**

Suggested Solution

We calculate the funds from operations in the following way:

Table 5.4 ***Statement of Funds from Operations (All figures in Rupees)***

M/s Johnny Lever and Sons		
Particulars	**Details**	**Amount**
Net Profit as per Profit & Loss Account		1,250,000
Add: Non-Cash and Non-Operating expenses		
Depreciation	250,000	
Loss on sale of machinery	500,000	750,000
		2,000,000
Less: Non-Operating incomes		
Profit on sale of Plant	500,000	
Interest income	400,000	
Dividend income	100,000	1,000,000
Funds from Operation		**1,000,000**

The above funds from operation represent the funds generated from the normal business operations of M/s Johnny Lever and Sons.

Statement of Changes in the Working Capital

In understanding the financial statements of a company, one of the first steps involved, is the study of the changes in the current financial position of the company, and the reasons for the changes.

We make an attempt at studying these changes and their causes by using the data contained in the summarized comparative balance sheet of Chottu Mottu Limited.

Example 5: Chottu Mottu

Table 5.5 ***Balance Sheet as of December 31, year 20X4 (All figures in Rupees Millions)***

Assets	December 31,20X4	December 31,20X3
Current assets		
Cash	19.05	10.87
Receivable	32.25	20.28
Loans and advances	42.58	33.82

(Contd.)

Table 5.5 ***(Contd.)***

Assets	**December 31,20X4**	**December 31,20X3**
Other current assets	17.2	15.93
Inventory	120.92	99.1
Total Current Assets	**232**	**180**
Fixed Assets		
Plant and equipment at cost	152	133
Less: Depreciation	71	60
Net Plant and equipment	**81**	**73**
Furniture & Fixtures at cost	14.5	8.6
Less: Depreciation	2	2.3
Net Furniture & Fixtures	**12.5**	**6.3**
Investments	**2**	
Intangible Assets		
Technical assistance fees	3	1
Less: Amortization	0.5	0.3
Net Intangible Assets	**2.5**	**0.7**
Total Assets	**330**	**260**
Liabilities & Capital		
Current Liabilities & Provisions		
Acceptance	4.74	3.02
Accounts payable	27.16	18.75
Advances against sales	26.6	20.28
Other liabilities	8.86	7.95
Interest accrued but not due on loans	2.64	2
Current Liabilities	**70**	**52**
Provisions:		
For taxation	25.55	20.45
Proposed dividend	2.25	2.25
For bonus	3.4	2.35
Other provision	3.8	2.95
Total Provisions	**35**	**28**
Total Current Liabilities & Provisions	**105**	**80**
Long-Term Liabilities		
Bank loans	40	32.14
Debentures 10.5%	25.5	25.5

(Contd.)

Table 5.5 **(Contd.)**

Assets	**December 31,20X4**	**December 31,20X3**
Loans from Financial Institutions	24.5	22.36
Total Long Term Liabilities	**90**	**80**
Total liabilities	**195**	**160**
Capital		
Authorized: 5,00,000 shares of ₹ 100 each	50	50
Issued, Subscribed and Paid Up: 3,73,100 shares of ₹ 100 each	37.31	37.31
Reserves and Surplus	97.69	62.69
Total Shareholders' funds	135	100
Liabilities & Capital	**330**	**260**

Note: *Furniture and fixtures costing ₹ 2 million, with accumulated depreciation of ₹ 1 million, were sold for cash at ₹ 2 million.*

The net change in working capital can be computed easily by subtracting the net working capital at the end of the year from the net working capital at the beginning of the year.

The increase of ₹ 27 million in the working capital of Chottu Mottu Limited, does not tell us much in terms of the operations of the business. This change could be the net result of changes in all the accounts covered by current items. There could have been qualitative changes resulting from the depletion of liquid items of current assets and increases in non-liquid items such as inventory. In order to clarify these possibilities, we try to analyze the changes in each of the working capital accounts.

Table 5.6 ***Statement of Changes in Working Capital (All figures in Rupees Millions)***

Chottu Mottu Limited		
	20X3	**20X4**
Current assets	180.00	232.00
Less: Current liabilities	80.00	105.00
Working capital	100.00	127.00
Working capital at the end of the 20X4		127.00
Working capital at the close of the 20X3		100.00
So, Increase in Working capital		**27.00**

A statement of changes in the working capital helps us in locating where these changes took place. At the first instance, we try to show the increases/decreases in the individual items and then, we try to classify them in terms of increases and decreases in the working capital. Since working capital is measured by subtracting current liabilities from current assets, any increase in the current assets and any decrease in the current liabilities cause an increase in the working capital. Similarly, any decrease in the current assets and any increase in the current liabilities represent a decrease in the working capital.

The statement of changes in the working capital of Chottu Mottu Limited below shows that the increase in the current assets amounted to ₹ 52 million, a major part of the increase arising out of cash, receivables and inventory. The decrease in the working capital came about mostly from the increased accounts payable, advances from customers and tax payable. The total amount from this increase in current liabilities amounted to ₹ 25 million. Thus, the net increase in the working capital was ₹ 27 million.

Table 5.7 ***Change in Working Capital (All figures in Rupees Millions)***

Chottu Mottu Limited						
Particulars	**20X4**	**20X3**	**Particulars**		**Working Capital**	
			Increase	**Decrease**	**Increase**	**Decrease**
Current assets						
Cash	19.05	10.87	8.18		8.18	
Receivable	32.25	20.28	11.97		11.97	
Loans and advances	42.58	33.82	8.76		8.76	
Other current assets	17.20	15.93	1.27		1.27	
Inventory	120.92	99.10	21.82		21.82	
Total Current Assets	**232.00**	**180.00**	**52.00**		**52.00**	
Current Liabilities & Provisions						
Acceptance	4.74	3.02	1.72			1.72
Accounts payable	27.16	18.75	8.41			8.41
Advances against sales	26.60	20.28	6.32			6.32
Other liabilities	8.86	7.95	0.91			0.91

(Contd.)

Table 5.7 ***(Contd.)***

Chottu Mottu Limited						
Particulars	**20X4**	**20X3**	**Particulars**		**Working Capital**	
			Increase	**Decrease**	**Increase**	**Decrease**
Interest accrued but not due on loans	2.64	2.00	0.68			0.64
Current Liabilities	**70.00**	**52.00**	**18.00**			**18.00**
Provisions:						
For taxation	25.55	20.45	5.10			5.10
Proposed dividend	2.25	2.25	0.00			0.00
For bonus	3.40	2.35	1.05			1.05
Other provision	3.80	2.95	0.85			0.85
Total Provisions	**35.00**	**28.00**	**7.00**			**7.00**
Total Current Liabilities & Provisions	**105.00**	**80.00**	**25.00**			**25.00**
Working Capital	**127.00**	**100.00**	**27.00**			

Changes in the Financial Position

An analysis of the changes in the working capital items could convey us insightful things. If it has increased, where has, the increased working capital been invested, and if it has decreased, from where have the funds been released. The profit & loss account gives the results of the operations and their impact on the position of the business.

As the title indicates, a fund flow statement integrates the profit and loss account with the balance sheet changes, tracing the flow of funds through the organization.

It is usually divided into the two logical divisions: The inflows during the periods and the outflows during the period. The division showing the sources of funds summarizes all those transactions which had the net effect of increasing the working capital. Uses of funds, on the other hand, deal with all those transactions, which had the effect of decreasing the working capital. The following figure captures the dynamics of a fund flow statement.

Now, that we have reasonable awareness with respect to the different items that constitute the fund flow statement, we continue the example of Chottu Mottu Limited and attempt to prepare its funds flow statement.

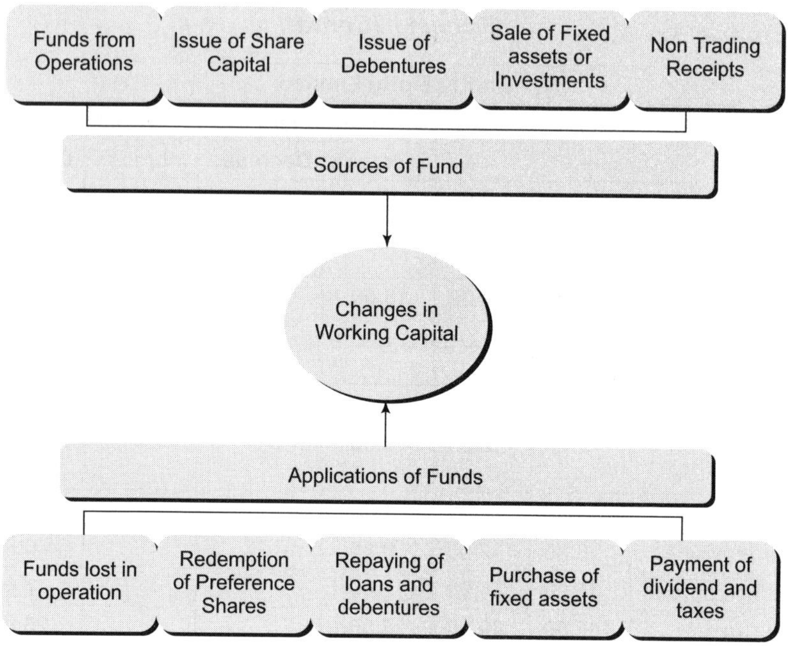

Fig. 5.4 ***Dynamics of Fund Flow Statement***

Fund Flow Statement Illustrated

From a comparative balance sheet and profit & loss account, we can obtain most of the information we require, for the preparation of a fund flow statement. We have studied that changes in the net working capital amount are caused by the changes in the non-working capital items. This could be easily seen from the summarized balance sheet of Chottu Mottu Limited.

We have seen that the net working capital amount increased by ₹ 27 million during 20X4, (refer to page no. 41-42). In other words, this implies that the sources of working capital from non-current sources should exceed non-current uses by ₹ 27 million.

The summarized balance sheet shown above marks out the net change in each account i.e., it does not show the receivables increases and decreases separately. Furniture and fixtures, for example, have increased by a net amount of ₹ 5.90 million. This increase shows an application of funds. In reality, the change in this account did not represent an acquisition of furniture alone. We purchased furniture and fixtures worth ₹ 7.90 million (an application of funds) and also sold of furniture and fixtures for cash at ₹ 2.00 million (a source of funds).

Table 5.8 ***Changes in Balance Sheet Items (All figures in Rupees Millions)***

			Change in balance sheet	
	20X4	**20X3**	**Source**	**Use**
Working capital[16]	127	100		27
Fixed Assets				
Plant and equipment at cost	152	133		19
Furniture and fixtures at cost	14.5	8.6		5.9
Investments	2	0		2
Intangible assets:				
Technical assistance fees	3	1		2
	298.5	**242.6**		**55.9**
Long-term Liabilities:				
Bank loans	40	32.14	7.86	
10.5% debentures	25.5	25.5		
Loans from financial institutions	24.5	22.36	2.14	
Depreciation and amortization				
Plant and equipment	71	60	11	
Furniture and fixtures	2	2.3		0.3
Technical assistance fees	0.5	0.3	0.2	
Share capital	37.31	37.31		
Reserves and surplus	97.69	62.69	35	
	298.5	**242.6**	**56.2**	**56.2**

Note: *Furniture and fixtures costing ₹ 2 million, with accumulated depreciation of ₹ 1 million, were sold for cash at ₹ 2 million.*

One can also observe from the above transaction that the construction of sources of funds as well as the uses of funds statement for the year needs additional information. Some of this additional information is available from the profit & loss account details. Some other information, like sales proceeds of assets are to be obtained from other records of the company such as notes to accounts, etc.

Here, we can see that operations were the major source of fund, which in turn, was used by the company for purchase of plant, furniture etc., and to pay dividends. It shows that the company's idea of CAPEX had, and will help it in earning, through operations.

[16]The components of current assets and current liabilities are clubbed under Working Capital as shown on page no. 39–41.

Table 5.9 Summarized Fund Flow Statement (All figures in Rupees Millions)

Chottu Mottu Limited		
Sources of funds:		
Funds from operations:		
Net Profit	55.00	
Less: Profit on sale of assets	1.00	
	54.00	
Add: Depreciation and amortization		
Plant	11.00	
Furniture and fixtures	0.70	
Technical assistance fee	0.20	
Total funds from operations		**65.90**
Funds generated from sale of furniture and fixtures		2.00
Additional bank loan		7.86
Additional loans from financial institutions		2.14
Total Sources of funds		**77.90**
Uses of funds		
Dividends	20.00	
Purchase of plant	19.00	
Purchase of furniture	7.90	
Investments	2.00	
Technical assistance fees	**2.00**	
Total non working capital uses		**50.90**
Working capital increase		**27.00**
Total Uses of funds		**77.90**

One can appreciate the company's financial position much better by using the above '*Funds Flow Statement*'. For example, one can easily start understanding the firm by raising simple issues such as:

1. What were the major sources of funds? What is the proportion of long-term sources vis-à-vis short-term sources? Are the sources sustainable in the future?
2. What are the major uses of funds? Are the funds for the long-term benefit of the company?
3. What are sources of funds that were used for the payment of dividends?

4. Is the firm approximately following a policy of using long-term sources for long-term purposes, and short-term sources for short-term requirements?

While analyzing companies, one should remember that these financial statements, including the balance sheet, profit & loss account and fund flow statement, are like pieces of a puzzle and hence, drawing extreme conclusions based on only one financial statement should be avoided.

To a large extent the 'Cash Flow Statement' is an extension of the (above discussed) 'Funds Flow Statement' – wherein the unit of analysis is 'Cash' instead of 'Funds' i.e., we delve into the "flow of cash" during a period (in a standardized presentation format as prescribed by the regulators). In the next chapter, we discuss the "Cash Flow Statement" in some detail.

6

CHAPTER

Preparing a Cash Flow Statement

Format

In a cash flow statement, the objective is to provide information on the changes during an accounting period, in cash and cash equivalents, and to classify the cash flows under three standard headings namely operating activities, investing activities, and financing activities.

Operating Activities

The idea is to convey to the user of the cash flow the cash generated solely as a result of the operating activities of the business, and hence, all the non-operating cash flows are adjusted to get purely the operating cash flow of the company. Examples of operating activities include: cash received from customers (cash inflow) and cash payments to suppliers and vendors (cash outflow). So, the profit adjusted for depreciation, gains and/or losses on sale of non-current assets, tax paid and working capital changes (such as increases or decreases in pre-paid expenses, inventories, receivables and payables), come under operating activities.

Investing Activities

Purchases of non-current assets and proceeds on the sale of non-current assets are called investing activities. Examples of cash outflow by way of investing activities include, purchase of machinery, land and long term investments. Examples of cash inflow by way of investing activities would be items such as disposal of real estate, old machinery and sale of long term investments.

Financing Activities

Examples of cash inflow due to financing activities would include issues of new debentures and issue of new equity shares. Repayment of loans, payment of interest (on loans) and dividends (to equity shareholders) would be good examples of cash outflow due to financing activities.

So, a cash flow statement is needed to identify and explain the difference between profits and cash, and thus, provides the user with a mechanism for providing additional information on its business activities and makes a better assessment of the current liquidity of a business.

Bholuram: Hey Finnova, can you tell me the basic difference between Cash Flow Statement and Fund Flow Statement?

Finnova: Why not Bholu, In a cash flow statement, the difference between the sources and application of cash represent the closing cash balance, whereas in a fund flow statement, the difference in sources and applications of funds, represents the increase or decrease in the working capital. Secondly, cash flow statement helps to assess the firm's capacity to meet short term obligations, whereas, funds flow statement helps to assess firm's capacity to meet its long term obligations.

Bholuram: Just a minute, Finnova. After assessing my stomach I feel there is an urgent need to fill it with short-term consumption inventory (stock in use). Hence please give me a break.

Preparing Cash Flow Statement: An Introduction

In this section, we will give you a brief introduction to the process of preparing a cash flow statement. All of the cash flow activities are supposed to be segregated into three heads; viz., operating activities, investing activities and financing activities. The sum of these activities reflects the net increase or decrease in the cash and cash equivalents.

Let us now understand each of the activities that form a part of the cash flow statement.

Operating Activities

There are two ways of calculating the cash flow from operating activities, viz., the direct method and the indirect method. The amount of cash provided by or used by operating activities is the same, no matter whichever method is used.

Under the direct method, gross receipts and gross payments of cash are disclosed, i.e. the amount of cash received from customers, and the amount of cash paid to suppliers and employees are disclosed. In other words, all transaction due to the operating activities resulting in cash inflows and outflows are tabulated in a systematic fashion.

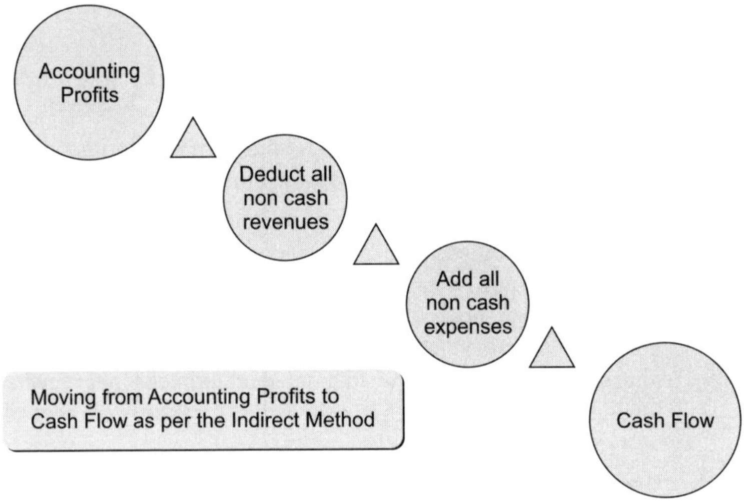

Fig. 6.1 ***Computing Cash Flow using Indirect Method***

Under the indirect method, the profit & loss account is adjusted for the effects of transactions of non-cash and non-operating nature. So, in this method, we start with the net income in the income statement. Cash transactions omitted from income are added. Non-cash transactions included in the income are removed. One can observe that this method is slightly similar to arriving at the funds from operations from a company's accounting profit, while preparing a funds flow statement (refer Chapter 5).

So to sum it up, we present below simple formats of direct and indirect methods of presenting 'Statement of Cash Flow'.

We present below a simple illustration of preparing a cash flow statement using Direct Method.

Bholuram: Hey Finnova, between direct and indirect methods, which one is better method of preparing cash flow from operating activities?

Finnova: Both the methods have their own advantages and shortcomings. Proponents of the direct method say that it shows the actual receipts and payments of the firm and hence, provides more information about the operations of the company.

On the other hand, the supporters of the indirect method claim this method to be more simpler and pinpoint the reasons behind the discrepancy between the profits and the actual cash flow.

In practice, most non-finance firms follow indirect method to compute cash flow from operating activities. While, all finance firms follow direct method to compute cash flow from operating activities.

Bholuram: Finnova!! You are my sweetu baby. Thank you so much.

Table 6.1 ***Direct Method***

Receipts from Debtors and Customers	XXXX	
Payments to Creditors and Suppliers	(XXXX)	
Payments towards Expenses	(XXXX)	
Taxes Paid	(XXXX)	**XXXX**
Cash Flow from Operating Activities (A)		**XXXX**
Proceeds from sale of Fixed Assets	XXXX	
Purchase of Fixed Assets and Investments	(XXXX)	
Dividend Received	XXXX	
Interest received	XXXX	XXXX
Cash Flow from Investing Activities (B)		**XXXX**
Proceeds from borrowings	XXXX	
Proceeds from issue of shares	XXXX	
Payment of long term borrowings	(XXXX)	

(Contd.)

Table 6.1 ***(Contd.)***

Payment of dividends	(XXXX)	XXXX
Cash Flow from Financing Activities (C)		**XXXX**
Net Cash Flow during the year = (A+B+C)		**XXXX**
Add: Opening Balance of Cash and Cash Equivalents		**XXXX**
Closing Balance of Cash		**XXXX**

Note: *The negative figures are presented in brackets.*

Table 6.2 ***Indirect Method***

To find out Cash from operations in **indirect method**, we should add back all the non-operating expenses to and subtract all the non operating incomes from the current year's profit and subsequently should give effects toward the changes in **Working Capital**.

Profit before taxation and extraordinary items XXXX		
Add:		
Adjustment (non-cash & non-operating items)		
Depreciation	**XXXX**	
Interest Expense	**XXXX**	
Interest Income	**(XXXX)**	
Dividend income	**(XXXX)**	
Operating Profit before Working Capital changes	XXXX	
Add: Decrease in Current Assets **(sources)**	XXXX	
Increase in Current Liability **(sources)**	XXXX	
Less: Increase in Current Assets **(application)**	(XXXX)	
Decrease in Current Liability **(application)**	(XXXX)	
Cash Generated from operations		**XXXX**
Less: Income Taxes paid		(XXXX)
Cash Flow from Operating Activities (A)		**XXXX**
Cash Flow from Investing Activities		
Proceeds from sale of Fixed Assets	XXXX	
Purchase of Fixed Assets and Investments	(XXXX)	
Dividend Received	XXXX	
Interest received	XXXX	**XXXX**

(Contd.)

Table 6.2 ***(Contd.)***

(B)		**XXXX**
Cash Flow from Financing Activities		
Proceeds from borrowings	**XXXX**	
Proceeds from issue of shares	**XXXX**	
Payment of long term borrowings	**(XXXX)**	
Payment of dividends	**(XXXX)**	
(C)		
Net Cash Flow during the year = **(A+B+C)**	**XXXX**	
	XXXX	
Add: Opening Balance of Cash and Cash Equivalents	**XXXX**	
Closing Balance of Cash	**XXXX**	

Example 6: Ram Software Limited[17]

The following are the list of Transactions for Ram Software Limited (RSL):

- On March 1, Ram & others invest ₹ 50,000 in cash in RSL.
- On March 2, Ram took a loan of ₹ 20,000 from Venugopal for RSL. Being a nice friend, Venugopal does not demand any interest on the loan amount and asks it to be repaid in six months' time.
- On March 3, RSL purchased for cash two computers, each costing ₹ 29,000.
- On March 4, RSL purchased supplies especially stationary for ₹ 6,000 on credit.
- On March 19, RSL completes its maiden sale of software to a retail store and receives a price of ₹ 12,000.
- On March 21, RSL pays ₹ 2,000 to its creditors for supplies.
- On March 29, RSL pays salaries to its employees, amounting to ₹ 4,000 and as office rent ₹ 1,200.
- On March 30, RSL delivers a software package for a shoe shop. The customer agrees to pay the price of ₹ 8,000 a week later.
- On March 31, Ram withdraws ₹ 3,500 for his personal use.

[17]Please refer Chapter 10 of *How to Read a Profit and Loss Statement-Second Edition* for going through the Ram Software Profit and Loss account.

At the end of the month, you are required to prepare its statement of cash flow.

Suggested Solution

The first and second transactions of raising owner's equity and taking a loan would be part of its financing activities as cash inflows.

The third transaction involving RSL purchasing two computers would be part of its investing activities cash outflow.

The fourth transaction would not lead to any change in its cash position and hence would not be part of its cash flow statement.

The next transaction on March 19, wherein RSL completes its maiden sale of software to a retail store and receives a price of ₹ 12,000 would be part of its operating cash inflow. On March 21, RSL pays ₹ 2,000 cash (part of its payables) to its supplier resulting in an operating cash outflow.

RSL pays salaries to its employees, amounting to ₹ 4,000 and as office rent ₹ 1,200 resulting in operating cash outflow.

RSL delivers a software package for a shoe shop worth ₹ 8,000 and the customer agrees to pay the price a week later. This transaction would result in neither a cash inflow nor a cash outflow and hence there would be no change in our statement of cash flow. On the other hand, accrual principle would have taken this transaction as an increase in the revenue of the company by a similar amount as part of its profit & loss account.

On March 31, the owner withdraws ₹ 3,500 from the profits of the company. We may consider this outflow of the company's profit as the dividend resulting in a cash outflow due to the firms financing activities.

A summary of all the above transactions would be:

Table 6.3 ***Ram Software Limited Statement of Cash Flow***

For the Period 1st to 31st March

(All figures in Rupees) (Using Direct Method)

Cash Flows from Operating Activities		
Cash received from customers	12,000	
Cash paid to suppliers, rent, and employees	(7,200)	
Net cash provided by operating activities (A)		**4,800**
Cash Flows from Investing Activities		
Purchase of office equipment	(58,000)	
Net cash provided by investing activities (B)		**(58,000)**

(Contd.)

Table 6.3 ***(Contd.)***

Cash Flows from Financing Activities		
Capital invested by owner, Equity	50,000	
Withdrawal by owner	(3,500)	
Loan	20,000	
Net cash provided by financing activities (C)		**66,500**
Net increase (decrease) in cash position (A+B+C)		**13,300**
Beginning cash balance		0
Cash balance at the end		13,300

Note: *The negative figures are presented in brackets.*

**Please note that the adjustment entries done based on the Matching principle (such as depreciation of fixed assets and expiry of inventory) would result in no change in the statement of cash flow.*

Bholuram: Hey Finnova, I am confused in separating items such as interest received, interest paid, dividend received and dividend paid into various activities.

Finnova: Don't worry Bholu, I will help you. Look, interest received on long term investments is an investing activity (even for a manufacturing firm), and any interest paid on loans and debts are financing activities. Similarly, dividend paid is a financing activity and dividend received is an investing activity.

Thus, if a financial enterprise (say, a bank or a brokerage dealer), dealing in securities, receives the dividend, then it will be an operating activity as its main operations is dealing in securities and not investing in it.

Now, can you tell me where will the fees you would pay me, go in my cash flow statement?

Bholuram: Of course, operating activities.

Finnova: Correct!! You are on track. ☺

Example 7: Shikari Shambu Security

Shikari Shambu was running an investigating agency, Shikari Shambu Security Services Limited. From the summary cash account of the firm, prepare the cash flow statement for the year ended 31st March 20X1.

Table 6.4 ***Summary Cash Account for the year ended 31st March 20X1 (All figures in Rupees)***

Shikari Shambu Security Services Ltd.			
Receipts	**Amount**	**Payments**	**Amount**
Cash balance as on 1.4.XX	10,000	Cash purchases during the year	200,000
Issue of equity shares	15,000	Factory expenses incurred	25,000
Issue of preference shares	15,000	Wages & salary paid	15,000
Cash sales for the period	230,000	Income tax paid	5,000
Sale of fixed assets	60,000	Dividend paid	15,000
		Repayment of loan	40,000
		Balance on 31.3.X1	30,000
Total	**330,000**	**Total**	**330,000**

Suggested Solution

As we read in the chapter, preparation of the cash flow statement can be done using two methods, viz., the direct method and the indirect method.

Only the calculation of cash flow from operating activities is different under both the methods, though the results are the same. We use the direct method here. The direct method requires the gross receipts and payments to be disclosed. Accordingly, our cash flow statement would be:

Table 6.5 ***Cash Flow Statement for the year ended 31st March 20X1 (All figures in Rupees)***

Shikari Shambu Security Services Ltd.	
Particulars	**Amount**
(A) Cash Flow From Operating Activities	
Receipt from customers (cash sales)	230,000
Payment to suppliers (cash purchases)	(200,000)
Payment for factory expenses	(25,000)
Payment for salary & wages	(15,000)
Income tax paid	(5,000)
Total (A)	**(15,000)**

(Contd.)

Table 6.5 ***(Contd.)***

Shikari Shambu Security Services Ltd.	
Particulars	**Amount**
(B) Cash Flow from Investing Activities	
Sale of fixed asset	60,000
Total (B)	**60,000**
(C) Cash Flow from Financing Activities	
Issue of equity shares	15,000
Issue of preference shares	15,000
Repayment of loan	(40,000)
Dividend paid	(15,000)
Total (C)	**(25,000)**
Total Cash Flow for the Period (A) + (B) + (C)	20,000
Add: Opening cash balance	10,000
Closing cash balance	**30,000**

Note: *The negative figures are presented in brackets.*

The company has shown a very weak performance wherein the cash has been generated through the sale of fixed assets and through issue of shares rather than through operations. The cash was basically utilized for repayment of loan and for paying the dividends.

7

CHAPTER

Interpretation of Cash Flow Statement

If you recall the discussion of matching principle in *How to Read a Profit and Loss Statement-Second Edition*, you would be clear with the concept that the expenses and revenues shown in the income statement are subject to lot of adjustments. Accountants instead of marking out the actual payments or receipts of cash, follow this matching concept. Hence, it would be impossible for anyone to analyze a company's financial position without knowing the exact inflow and outflow of cash. For this, we need the help of a cash flow statement. This statement also helps by presenting the *flow of cash* during a period into three types – operating activities, investing activities and financing activities.

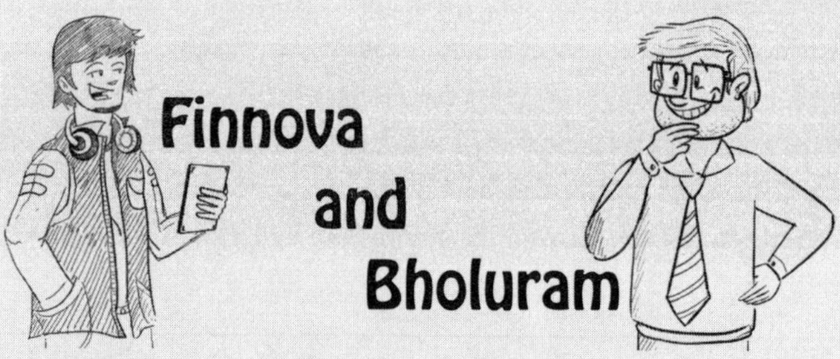

Bholuram: Finnova, what could be the possible examples of operating activities, investing activities and financial activities?

Finnova: *Operating activities* of a business mean the daily activities of a firm in generating revenue, marketing its products and service offerings, administering payroll and maintaining its facilities.

Revenue can be generated through either selling manufactured goods or selling added services along with it. Suppose a bakery shop sells breads purchased from a wholesaler, but also would want to sell pastries made in its own shop.

Marketing products may be in the form of some free sachets of a new shampoo launched in the market to every household in the prospering metro cities and towns.

Administrative activities may include expenses on managerial services for huge administration requirements. Hence, only big companies are capable of bearing such activities via qualified professionals.

General activities may include expenses such as electricity bill payments, rent, water supplies, insurance and licenses. For example, a textile industry would need to keep its facilities up-to-date so that its equipments remain clean and in working order.

Whereas, *Investing activities* include the purchase or sale of long-term investments such as land, shop, etc.; equipments used in the business such as machines, computers, water pumps, and so on. These activities increase in cash outflow because huge amount of cash is required to carry them on.

On the other hand, *Financing activities* may include a) sources of cash inflow such as issuing equity shares to investors and getting cash in return; issuing debt and slowly paying off the interest or b) uses the existing cash with the firm in activities such as retiring debt which means that the firm chooses to pay its debt soon using enough cash and reduces its liabilities. In this category, also fall the repurchasing of stocks; which means that a firm buys shares back at higher price including trading fees, etc. Paying dividends to the shareholders supports the cash outflow further. Hence small and large businesses generally use financing activities to support operations and strategic initiatives.

Bholuram: This is quite interesting!

In the recent times of high company failures, cash flow statement has come to acquire a significance of its own. The key reason is very simple - whereas it is comparatively easier to tamper with the Income Statement and Balance Sheet items of a company (with the help of innovative accounting practices), the manipulation of the cash balances has proved to be a much tougher exercise. So, it is very difficult to manipulate a statement of cash flow.

Let us have a glimpse of Cash Flow Statement from a listed company's annual report, namely Vishnu Chemicals Limited. The company is a mid-sized manufacturer of inorganic chemicals based in Andhra Pradesh.

Table 7.1 ***Cash flow statement of Vishnu Chemicals Limited for the year ended 31st March 20X3 (all Figures in Rupees Millions)***

Financial Year	FY20X3 (12m)	FY20X2 (12m)
A. CASH FLOWS FROM OPERATING ACTIVITIES		
Net Profit after Tax and Extraordinary items	730	850
Adjustments for:		
Depreciation	1220	1130
Other Adjustments (largely, interest and tax related)	3740	3520
Operating profit before working Capital changes	**5690**	**5500**
Adjustments for:		
(Increase)/Decrease in Trade and Other Receivables	780	(70)
Increase)/Decrease in Inventories	(1120)	(1460)
Increase/(Decrease) in Trade Payables & Other Current Liabilities	790	2300
(Increase)/Decrease on Loans & Advances	(380)	(1170)
Cash deficit from Operations	**70**	**(400)**
Net Cash Flow from operating activities (A)	**5760**	**5110**
B. CASH FLOWS FROM INVESTING ACTIVITIES:		
Purchase of Fixed Assets	(40)	(90)
Sale Proceeds from Fixed Assets	10	-
Purchase of Investments	(10)	-
Capital Work-in-progress	(1490)	(1810)
Interest Received from Investments	110	110
Net Cash used in investing activities (B)	**(1420)**	**(1790)**
C. CASH FLOWS FROM FINANCING ACTIVITIES:		
Increase (Decrease) in Preference Share Capital	-	(1000)
Proceeds from long-term borrowings	-	3000
Repayment of term liabilities	(3090)	(4020)
Increase in Bank Borrowings Working Capital	2400	420
Other Un Secured Loans	(410)	1640
Interest Paid	(3290)	(3150)
Net Cash used in financing activities (C)	**(4390)**	**(3110)**
Net increase / Decrease in cash and cash equivalents i.e., (A) + (B) + (C)	**(50)**	**210**
Cash and cash equivalents as at the beginning of the year	990	780
Cash and Cash equivalents as at the end of the year	940	990

Note: *The negative figures are presented in brackets.*

After seeing the above Cash Flow Statement, few things for sure are understood:

1. The above Cash Flow Statement is for the FY20X3, which has been compared with its preceding FY20X2. Hence, one can say that it covers two accounting periods.
2. The cash flows (i.e. cash receipts and cash payments) has been categorized under three different activities:
   - *Operating* Activities
   - *Investing* Activities and
   - *Financing* Activities
3. Finally, it also shows opening and closing cash positions of the accounting periods (refer to last rows).

Thus, a Cash Flow Statement helps to answer the following type of questions:

- How did cash position change, compared to the accounting profits reported based on the income statements?
- Did the firm issue/redeem any share capital during the period?
- How was the expansion in the plant and machinery financed?
- How much money was borrowed during the year?
- From where did the company bring in and spend out the cash?
- What is the company using extra cash for?
- Has the company's operating activities generated enough cash to support the payment of interest, dividends and fund its CAPEX[18] (Capital Expenditure) during the period?
  - If NO, then how have the payments for interest, dividends and CAPEX been dealt with?
  - If YES, then how was the excess cash dealt with?

In the next few pages – we answer exactly these queries for Vishnu Chemicals. We also do the same for Hindustan Unilever Limited, the Fast Moving Consumer Goods Giant at the end of this chapter.

[18]Capital expenditures (CAPEX) are expenditures creating future benefits. A capital expenditure is incurred when a business spends money either to buy fixed assets or to add to the value of an existing fixed asset with a useful life that extends beyond the taxable year. Example: Acquisition of fixed assets. It has been discussed in *How to Read a Profit and Loss Statement-Second Edition*, in Chapter 4, footnote no. 4.

Bholuram: Hey, Finnova, why is the adjustment in the above table shown as an Increase/Decrease in Trade & Other Receivables and why not as an adjustment for just Trade & Other Receivables?

Finnova: Nice question from you Bholu!

Well, if you notice Bholu, the cash flows from the operating activities are made based on the principle revenue generating activities of the firm. Cash flow from operating activities can show either of the two methods- Direct and Indirect method, depending on the firm's choice.

The *Direct method* illustrates the actual major classes of operating cash received from customers and cash paid to suppliers/ employees, income tax paid or depreciation/amortization are organized and presented in the Cash Flow. To sum it up, *Direct Method* tabulates each of these operating transactions, summarizes them and presents it.

While, the *Indirect method* uses the firm's existing balance sheet and income statement to create its cash flow from operations. Thus, it begins with the net profit and adjusts it for those revenue and expense items that did not at all show up in the operating cash receipts or cash payments in the current accounting period to arrive at net cash flow from operating activities.

The answer to your question is that Vishnu Chemicals has used the *Indirect Method* by referring to the balance sheet and income statement of the current period.

Bholuram: You've collaged it all into such a nice frame ☺

Now another query arrives in my mind… What is the difference between *Net Operating Cash Flows* and *Net income*?

Finnova: Based on GAAP, the Net income (net profit after tax) is considered as the profit after all expenses have been accounted for.

But, cash from operating activities is the cash increase from just the operating activities of the business, i.e. the cash flow. It does not include buying and selling assets (investing activities) or borrowing / paying back debt or money received from issuing stock (financing activities).

Manufacturing Companies use the indirect method of preparing the cash flow statement where they begin with net income and then add / subtract i.e., make adjustments. Cash is the sail of a company's ship. If a company doesn't generate cash over the long term, then it is definitely sinking.

Table 7.2 ***Analysis of Cash Flow Statement of Vishnu Chemicals Limited (all figures in Rupees Millions)***

Analysis Items	FY20X3 (12m)	FY20X2 (12m)
What are the Major Sources of Cash during the period?	Cash from Operations 5760	Cash from Operations 5080
	Decrease in Cash Balance 60	Loans Taken 1040
What are the Major Uses of Cash during the period?	Capex 1540	Capex 1900
	Loan Repaid 1100	Redemption of Preference Shares 1000
	Interest Paid 318	Increase in its Cash Balance 180
		Interest Paid 3100
Is Capex > Depreciation during the period?	Yes	Yes
	1540 > 1220	1900 > 1130
Is Cash from Operations > Capex + Interest Paid + Dividend?	Yes, but No Dividend paid	Yes, but No Dividend paid
If No for the above question, then how was the funding done?	Not Applicable	Not Applicable
If Yes for the above question, then where has the money gone?	Repayment of Term. Loans	Redeeming the Preference Shares
Bankruptcy Rating (on a Scale of 1 to 10, where	6.5	6

(*Contd.*)

Table 7.2 *(Contd.)*

Analysis Items	FY20X3 (12m)	FY20X2 (12m)
in 1 stands for high hazard of Bankruptcy and 10 stands for near zero risk of bankruptcy)		
Bankruptcy Rating	Operations have improved & are much more than interest paid. They are also very stable. Firm has also started repaying its Long Term Borrowings. Lack of Dividend indicates a focus of the management on slowly deleveraging itself and reducing the say of its lenders. It seems, they have possibly realized the need to stop playing in the hands of bankers; and consolidate their existing space. Thus, future looks interesting to watch … ☺	

As you can see from the above analysis, one can observe that a lot of important information and cues for above types of questions get answered by analyzing a statement of cash flow.

The Need for a Cash Flow Statement

The need for a cash flow statement also stems out of the inherent limitations of the balance sheet and the profit and loss account. Some of the limitations of these statements are:

- concentrate only on the accounting profits of the firm. Hence, the cash component, which provides liquidity to the firm and is integral to the survival of the business, is not given due importance.[19]
- There is no clear demarcation between the operational and non-operational aspects of the business. Hence, it may become relatively

[19]The Balance Sheet paints a static picture of the business. It provides information about the business at a particular point of time, and fails to convey the dynamism and the movement in the various assets and liabilities of the business.

difficult for a user of the financial statement to clearly identify the fundamental earning capability of a company.

- There are a variety of ways and means available to compute certain items of the P&L account and the Balance Sheet such as depreciation, value of inventory etc., which leads to confusion and a scope for manipulation of figures. Items of the cash flow are comparatively standardized, not prone for manipulation and thus, give a clearer picture.

Given the above positives, the cash flow statement provides the firm with detailed information regarding the flow of cash in business and the current state of liquidity that the firm is in. It is also helpful to other stakeholders of the business such as investors, creditors and shareholders, who get a sense of the amount of risk and return to be expected from the business. It also clearly demarcates the activities of the business into operational, investing and financing activities to convey a simpler and easily digestible picture to the user. Thus, one can say that a cash flow statement gives rich information not only regarding its solvency position but also relationship between a company's profitability with its various types of activities (both operational and non-operational).

Cash and Cash Equivalents

When we prepare a cash flow statement, we seek to track the movement of cash and its equivalents. The items that fit the description of cash and cash equivalents are as follows:

- Cash, as we understand in general terms, i.e. the amount of currency available with us
- Demand deposits with the bank, i.e. any amount deposited with the bank that is free to withdraw whenever we so desire. (Examples: Saving account and current account with Banks).
- Short term, highly liquid investments that can be readily converted to cash. (Example: a 15-day bank fixed deposit).

Example 5:

Hindustan Unilever Limited is an Indian fast moving consumer goods company. It is owned by the Anglo-Dutch company, Unilever. Let us analyze the following cash flow statement of the Hindustan Unilever Limited (HUL) taken from its annual report for the financial year 20X3.

Table 7.3 Cash Flow Statement of Hindustan Unilever Limited (All figures in Rupees Millions)

Financial Year	20X3 (12m)	20X2 (12m)
A. CASH FLOW FROM OPERATING ACTIVITIES		
Net Profit before tax and extraordinary items and tax	44,600	35,080
Adjustments for:		
Depreciation and amortization expense	2,510	2,340
Other Adjustments (largely, interest and tax related)	(15,360)	(9,110)
Operating profit before working capital changes	**31,760**	**28,310**
(Increase)/decrease in trade receivables	(1,490)	840
(Increase)/decrease in short term loans & advances	(1,400)	(650)
(Increase)/decrease in other current assets		0
(Increase)/decrease in long term loans & advances	(120)	(220)
Increase/(decrease) in trade payables	4,930	(2,470)
Increase/(decrease) in long term provisions	460	10
Increase/(decrease) in short term provision	50	270
Increase/(decrease) in other current liabilities	740	(60)
Increase/(decrease) in other long term liabilities	1,500	1,200
Increase/(decrease) in inventories	(390)	2,080
Cash From Operations	**4,290**	**1,000**
Net cash inflow/(outflow) from operating activities (A)	**36,050**	**29,310**
B. CASH FLOW FROM INVESTING ACTIVITIES		
Purchase of tangible/intangible assets	(4,410)	(2,810)
Sale proceeds of tangible assets	10	70
Purchase of non-current investment	(3,260)	(10)
Purchase of current investments	(158,540)	(139,660)
Dividend Received	380	170
Interest Received	2,140	1,340
Others Adjustments	164,320	135,740
Net cash outflow from investing activities B	**630**	**(5,140)**
C. CASH FLOW FROM FINANCING ACTIVITIES		
Dividend paid	(35,580)	(15,090)

(Contd.)

Table 7.3 ***(Contd.)***

Financial Year	20X3 (12m)	20X2 (12m)
Dividend distribution tax paid	(5,790)	(2,450)
Addition to unpaid dividend accounts	(170)	(30)
Interest paid	(260)	(20)
Monies borrowed for long term purposes	80	
Monies borrowed for short term purposes	160	
Proceeds from share allotment	70	340
Net cash inflow from financing activities C	**(41,470)**	**(17,260)**
Net increase/decrease in cash and cash equivalents (i.e., A + B + C)	(4,800)	6,920
Cash and cash equivalents at the beginning of the year	9,420	2,500
Cash and cash equivalents at the end of the year	**4,620**	**9,430**

Note: *The negative figures are presented in brackets*

Suggested Solution

Here we present you the simple format for analyzing a cash flow statement of a company:

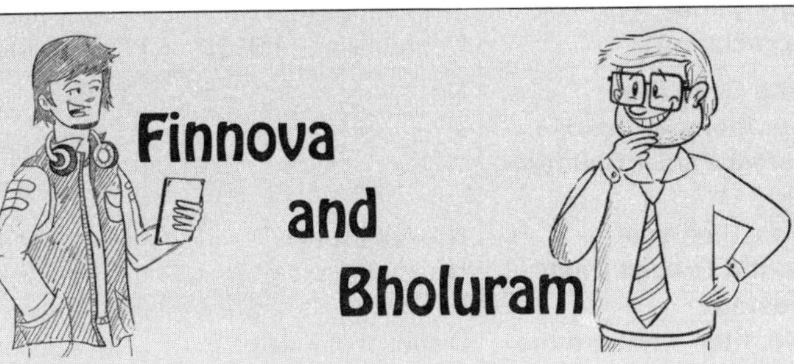

Bholuram: Finnova, why is interest received disclosed under investing activities? Please explain.

Finnova: Manufacturing firms tend to invest the excess funds with them for earning some additional income. Thus, Interest collected on loans advanced to other organizations becomes the part of investing activities of a statement of cash flow.

Bholuram: Interest Income Received ... is visible in Hindustan Unilever's figures, which means the firm is investing the excess funds available to earn some additional money.

Table 7.4 ***Analysis of Cash Flow Statement of Hindustan Unilever Limited (all figures in Rupees Millions)***

Analysis Points	FY 20X3	FY 20X2
What are the Major Sources of Cash during the period?	Cash from Operations (36,040) Disposal of Fixed Assets (6,490) Decrease in Cash Balance (4,800) Borrowings (250)	Cash from Operations (29,310) Disposal of Fixed Assets (1,450) Issue of Stock Options (340)
What are the Major Uses of Cash during the period?	Dividends (41,500) Capex (4,410) Purchase of Investments (1,450) Interest Paid (260)	Dividends (17,550) Capex (2,810) Purchase of Investments (3,780) Increase in Cash Balance (6,920)
How does the Cash Flow from Operations (CFO) compare to Net Profit figures of the firm?	CFO > 0; CFO < Net Profit CFO increases Due to - Depreciation (2,510) - A/P Up (4,930) But CFO decreases due to, - A/R Down (1,490)	CFO > 0; CFO < Net Profit CFO increases Due to - Depreciation (2,330) - Inventories Down (2,080) But CFO decreases due to, - A/P Down (2,450)
Is the Cash From Operations > Capex? **Is the Capex > Depreciation?**	Yes, very comfortably Yes, Capex (4,410) > Depreciation (2,510)	Yes, very comfortably Yes, Capex (2,810) > Depreciation (2,330)
Is the Cash From Operations > Capex + Interest Paid + Dividend Paid? **If Yes, then where was the Excess Cash Invested?** **If No, then what are the Sources of Cash for payment of Dividends + Interest Paid + Capex**	No Not Applicable Disposal of Fixed Assets	Yes Purchase of Investments Not Applicable
Other Items	Issue of Stock Options (70)	Interest Paid (20)
Trends **Income Before Tax** **CFO**	Increasing, Steadily (44,600)	Positive (35,070) Positive (29,310)

(Contd.)

Table 7.4 ***(Contd.)***

Analysis Points	FY 20X3	FY 20X2
Capex **Dividends** **Net Borrowing** **Working Capital**	Increasing, Steadily (36.040) Increasing, Steady (4,410) Increasing, Huge Jump (41,500) Very low borrowings Mixed Signals, A/P increased whereas A/R trend reversed	Decent for a large company (2,810) Stable, Huge (17,550) Near Zero Borrowings Decreasing, both inventories and A/P showing reverse trend

Note: *A/P = Accounts Payable*
A/R = Accounts Receivable

We end our analysis by stating that the Trends look absolutely brilliant. Perhaps, this is the reason why the parent firm, Unilever, want to own all of the company. It has very high profitability, with healthy and growing CFO. This would be a dream for someone to be part of such a solid company in a mature industry. The company seems to have paid a special dividend resulting in large outflow during the latest year i.e., FY20X3. However, it does not make any big difference to the company. Thus, we end by stating that HUL has all the traits of a large player in a mature business (using its excess funds for investment purposes). (Rating: 10 on a Bankruptcy scale of 1 to 10, wherein 10 stands for near zero risk of Bankruptcy.)

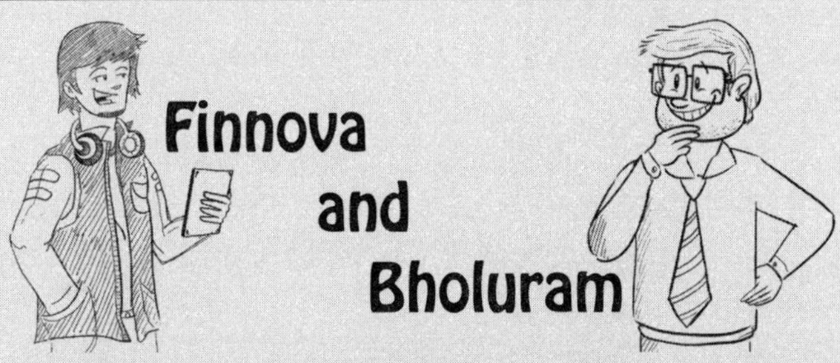

Bholuram: Finnova, so far we have discussed about the three main financial statements. Which one is best?

Finnova: See, Bhola, there is no doubt in saying that each of the financial statements is important from the perspective of its analysts. For example,

- Auditors mainly audit the balance sheet, hence that is their greatest interest.
- An investor analyses the share value based on cash flows, so they are mostly interested in the statement of cash flows.
- Managers are responsible for pacing up the business by analyzing its profit/loss figures, so they are likely to be more interested in the income statement.

Each one also provides different type of information and insights. However, the utility of each of these individual financial statements goes up drastically, when they are combined intelligently with other information, both qualitative and quantitative. And that is what we need to focus on.

Bholuram: Yes of course… that is absolutely logical, Finnova ☺.

8
CHAPTER
Solved illustrations

As we have read through the preparation and interpretation of a cash flow statement, it would be better to surf through some useful illustration to brush up our understanding of the same.

Example 8: Munna Bhai Enterprises

From the information provided by Munna Bhai Enterprises, we can prepare a statement of changes in working capital and the fund flow statement for the year.

Table 8.1 ***Balance Sheet as at 31st March 20X3 (All figures in Rupees)***

Munna Bhai Enterprises					
Assets	**Year 20X2**	**Year 20X3**	**Liabilities**	**Year 20X2**	**Year 20X3**
Current Assets	**Amount**	**Amount**	**Current Liabilities**	**Amount**	**Amount**
Cash in Hand	10,000	2,000	Sundry Creditors	3,00,000	2,00,000
Bank Balances	20,000	8,000	Provision for Taxes	10,000	15,000
Sundry Debtors	2,10,000	1,80,000	Proposed Dividend	50,000	60,000
Stock	4,00,000	4,50,000			
Total Current Assets	**6,40,000**	**6,40,000**	**Total Current Liabilities**	**3,60,000**	**2,75,000**
Fixed Assets					
Fixed Assets	8,00,000	11,00,000			

(Contd.)

Table 8.1 ***(Contd.)***

Munna Bhai Enterprises					
Assets	**Year 20X2**	**Year 20X3**	**Liabilities**	**Year 20X2**	**Year 20X3**
Current Assets	**Amount**	**Amount**	**Current Liabilities**	**Amount**	**Amount**
Less : Accumulated Depreciation	160,000	270,000			
Total Fixed Assets	**640,000**	**830,000**			
Other Assets			**Shareholders' Funds**		
Investments	160,000	670,000	Equity Share Capital	980,000	1,715,000
			General Reserves	100,000	150,000
Total Other Assets	**160,000**	**670,000**	**Total Shareholders' Funds**	**1,080,000**	**1,865,000**
Total Assets	**1,440,000**	**2,140,000**	**Total Liabilities**	**1,440,000**	**2,140,000**

It is also known that machinery costing ₹ 100,000, with an accumulated depreciation of ₹ 30,000 was sold for ₹ 60,000.

Suggested Solutions

By this time, it is quite clear that we can easily prepare a statement of changes in working capital, if we are able to identify the current assets and the current liabilities. This is because the statement of changes in working capital presents the net change in the working capital for the period. Our statement of changes in working capital for Munna Bhai Enterprises is as follows:

Table 8.2 ***Statement of Changes in Working Capital (All figures in Rupees)***

Munna Bhai Enterprises				
Particulars	**Year 20X2**	**Year 20X3**	**Increase in Working Capital**	**Decrease in Working Capital**
Current Assets:				
Closing Stock	400,000	450,000	50,000	
Sundry Debtors	210,000	180,000		30,000

(Contd.)

Table 8.2 *(Contd.)*

Munna Bhai Enterprises				
Particulars	**Year 20X2**	**Year 20X3**	**Increase in Working Capital**	**Decrease in Working Capital**
Cash in Hand	10,000	2,000		8,000
Bank Balance	20,000	8,000		12,000
Total (A)	**640,000**	**640,000**		
Current Liabilities:				
Sundry Creditors	300,000	200,000	100,000	
Provision For taxes	10,000	15,000		5,000
Proposed Dividends	50,000	60,000		10,000
Total (B)	**360,000**	**275,000**		
Working Capital (A) – (B)	280,000	365,000		
Increase in Working Capital	85,000			85,000
Total	**365,000**	**365,000**	**150,000**	**150,000**

Now, before preparing the fund from operation statement and the fund flow statement, we have to calculate the amount of depreciation charged for the year and also the amount of profit or loss on account of sale of machinery. For this, we need to prepare a machinery account in the following manner.

Table 8.3 ***Changes in the Machinery Account for the Year 20X3 (All figures in Rupees)***

Munna Bhai Enterprises	
Particulars	**Amount**
Balance of Fixed Assets as at 20X2	800,000
Less: Cost of Machinery sold	100,000
Balance in fixed assets group after sale	700,000
Amount of Fixed assets as at 20X3	1,100,000
Difference being additional purchase in the Year	400,000

The written down value of the machinery is the cost minus the accumulated depreciation up to the point of sale. The sale price of the machinery minus the written down value of the machinery sold was ₹ 60,000 – [₹ 100,000 – ₹ 30,000]. Loss on sale of machinery comes to ₹ 10,000.

Based upon the same logic, we have to calculate the amount of depreciation for the year.

Table 8.4 **Depreciation for the Year 20X3 (All figures in Rupees)**

Munna Bhai Enterprises	
Particulars	**Amount**
Opening Balance of Accumulated Depreciation	160,000
Less: Accumulated depreciation of machinery sold	30,000
Balance in the accumulated depreciation account	130,000
Closing balance as on 20X3	270,000
Difference being depreciation for the year	140,000

Table 8.5 **Funds From Operations for the Year 20X3 (All figures in Rupees)**

Munna Bhai Enterprises	
Particulars	**Amount**
Profit for the Year (Increase in General reserves)	50,000
Add: Depreciation	140,000
Non-operational activity (loss on machine)	10,000
Funds From Operations	200,000

Table 8.6 **Fund Flow Statement for the Year 20X3 (All figures in Rupees)**

Munna Bhai Enterprises	
Particulars	**Amount**
Sources:	
Funds from Operation	200,000
Proceeds from Sale of Machinery	60,000
Proceeds from Issue of Shares	735,000
Total (A)	**995,000**
Applications:	
Purchase of Machinery	400,000
Purchase of Investment	510,000
Increase in Working Capital	85,000
Total (B)	**995,000**

We can say that the enterprise has been using its funds in assets that would generate the funds in future. The enterprise is good at managing its working capital fund and also in generating funds from operations.

Example 10: Mungeri Lal & sons

Mungeri Lal was a farmer, managing a small farm. He saw no future in traditional cultivation (using chemicals) and shifted to organic farming (under contract) for a big multinational. His last two year's financial statements are given below:

Table 8.7 ***Balance Sheet as at 31st March 20X3 (All figures in Rupees)***

Mungeri Lal & Sons					
Assets	**Year 20X3**	**Year 20X2**	**Liabilities**	**Year 20X3**	**Year 20X2**
Current Assets	**Amount**	**Amount**	**Current Liabilities**	**Amount**	**Amount**
Cash & Bank	20,000	15,000	Sundry Creditors	10,000	0
Sundry Debtors	20,000	15,000			
Stock	15,000	10,000			
Total Current Assets	**55,000**	**40,000**	**Total Current Liabilities**	**10,000**	**0**

Mungeri Lal & Sons					
Assets	**Year 20X3**	**Year 20X2**	**Liabilities**	**Year 20X3**	**Year 20X2**
Fixed Assets			**Long Term Liabilities**		
Land	80,000	70,000	Loan from Bank of Rajasthan	30,000	15,000
Total Fixed Assets	**80,000**	**70,000**	**Total Long Term Liabilities**	**30,000**	**15,000**
			Shareholders' Funds		
			Capital	95,000	95,000
			Total Shareholders' Funds	**95,000**	**95,000**
Total Assets	**1,35,000**	**1,10,000**	**Total Liabilities**	**1,35,000**	**1,10,000**

Based on the information given above,please prepare the fund flow statement for him.

Table 8.8 ***Profit & Loss Account for the year ended March 20X3 (All figures in Rupees)***

Mungeri Lal & Sons		
Particulars	**Amount**	**Amount**
Sales		10,000
Less: Cost of goods sold		
Material Consumed	6,000	
Gross margin		**4,000**
Less: Other operating expenses	4,000	
Profit		**Nil**

Suggested Solution

Based on the above data, we go ahead and prepare the fund flow statement of Mungeri Lal & Sons:

Table 8.9 ***Fund Flow Statement for the Year 20X3 (All figures in Rupees)***

Mungeri Lal & Sons	
Particulars	**Amount**
(A) Sources:	
Funds From Operation	Nil
Loan from Bank of Rajasthan	15,000
Total	**15,000**
(B) Applications:	
Land	10,000
Change in Working Capital (Balancing Figure)	5,000
Total	**15,000**

Here we can see that the company's source of funds has been through bank finance, which has been used for purchase of land and in maintaining its working capital. It doesn't show a good sign. The company's operation is contributing nothing towards the firm funds requirement.

Now let us move on to some live illustrations of Cash Flow Statements of three large textile companies with retail focus – Provogue Limited, Arvind Limited, and Raymond Limited.

Illustration 1 ***Consolidated cash flow statement of Provogue Limited for the year ended 31 st March 20X2***

(in Millions)

Particulars	Year ended	Year ended
A. CASH FLOW FROM OPERATING ACTIVITIES:	**31.03.20X2**	**31.03.20X1**
Net profit before tax Adjustments for:	258	209
Depreciation	138	281
Others Adjustments	175	177
Operating profit before working capital changes	**571**	**668**
Adjustments for:		
Decrease/(Increase) in Trade receivables	(1019)	(649)
Decrease/(Increase) in Inventories	(321)	(942)
Decrease/(Increase) in Other current assets	13	(40)
Decrease/(Increase) in Short-term loans and advances	(107)	(1168)
Decrease/(Increase) in Long-term loans and advances	221	1192
Decrease/(Increase) in Other non-current assets	60	(57)
Increase/(Decrease) in Trade payables	229	(11)
Increase/(Decrease) in Other current liabilities	70	428
Increase/(Decrease) in Long-term provisions	(0)	1
Increase/(Decrease) in Short term provisions	(1)	13
Increase/(Decrease) in Other long- term liabilities	(3)	57
Cash generated from/(used in) operations	**(287)**	**(509)**
Direct taxes paid	(150)	(154)
Net cash flow from/(used in) operating activities (A)	**(437)**	**(663)**
B. CASH FLOW FROM INVESTING ACTIVITIES:		
Purchase of fixed assets	(153)	(2708)
Sale of fixed assets	10	217
Capital work in progress	17	2019
Purchase of non-current investments	(402)	(193)
Sale of non-current investments	2	1
Purchase of current investments	(846)	(6830)
Sale of current investments	1174	6550
Redemption/maturity of bank deposits (having maturity of more than 3 months)	(32)	(36)
Interest income	130	141

(Contd.)

Illustration 1 *(Contd.)*

Particulars	Year ended	Year ended
Dividend income	10	24
Net cash flow from/(used in) investment activities (B)	**(89)**	**(814)**
C. CASH FLOW FROM FINANCING ACTIVITIES:		
Proceeds from issue of shares to minority shareholders of subsidiaries	41	2183
Proceeds from share application money		(5)
Proceeds from borrowings - short term (net)	629	698
Proceeds from borrowings - long term (net)	187	(1165)
Finance Cost	(354)	(366)
Dividend Paid including tax thereon	(33)	(27)
Net cash flow from/(used in) financing activities (C)	**469**	**1318**
Net increase/(decrease) in cash and cash equivalents (A+B+C)	**(57)**	**(159)**
Cash and cash equivalents at the beginning of the year	**163**	**311**
Others Adjustments	**(32)**	**11**
Cash and Cash Equivalents at the end of the year	**73**	**163**

Analysis 1 ***Statement of Cash Flow Analysis of Provogue Limited (FY20X1–X2 compare to FY 20XX)***

	FY 20X2	FY 20X1	FY 20XX
What are the Major Sources of Cash during the period?	Net Borrowings (81) Proceeds from Investments (6) Cash Balanced Down (6)	Issue of Shares (218) Cash Balanced Down (16)	
What are the Major Uses of Cash during the period?	Loss from Operations (-44) Capex (15) Interest Paid (35) Dividend (3)	Capex (71) Loss from Operations (-66) Repayment of Loan (49) Purchase of Investments (10) Interest Paid (37) Dividend (3)	

(Contd.)

Analysis 1 *(Contd.)*

	FY 20X2	FY 20X1	FY 20XX
How does the Cash Flow from Operations (CFO) compare to Net Profit figures of the firm?	CFO < 0; CFO < Net Income Due to - Depreciation 14 But, - A/R Up 102 - Inventories Up 32	CFO < 0; CFO < Net Income Due to - Depreciation 28 But, - Inventories Up 94 - A/R Up 65	-
Is the Cash From Operations > Capex? **Is the Capex > Deprecation?**	No, CFO is negative Capex (15) = Depreciation (14)	No, CFO is negative Capex (71) >> Depreciation (28)	
Is the Cash From Operations > Capex + Interest Paid + Dividend Paid? **If Yes, then where was the Excess Cash Invested?** **If No, then what are the Sources of Cash for payment of Dividends + Interest Paid + Capex**	No	No	
Excess Cash Invested	NA	NA	
Sources of Cash for Dividends + Interest Paid + Capex	Borrowings	Issue of Shares	
Other Items	Issue of Shares (4)		
Trends **Income Before Tax** **CFO** **Capex** **Dividends** **Net Borrowing** **Working Capital**	Increasing, Stable (26) Increasing, Marginally (-44) Decreasing, Steeply (15) Stable, Notional amount (3) Net Borrower (81) Increased, All CA Use, CL Source	Decreasing, Stable (21) Decreasing, Marginally (-66) Decreasing, Steep Fall (71) Stable, Notional amount (3) Net Repayer (49) Increased, All CA use	Decreasing, Steadily (33) Negative, Steady (-60) Steady State (201) Stable (4) Net Borrower (146) Increased, All CA Use, CL Source

This company is continuously draining cash. Operating Cash Flows have always been negative. Primarily, with more and more *funds getting stuck in working capital items such as receivables and inventories.* Surprisingly, the company is able to fund itself with the borrowings (latest year) and the issue of shares (last year) reflecting *confidence in the model by both the long-term capital investors.* Perhaps, they are waiting for some major event (such as, takeover or favorable court rulings). (Rating: 2 on a Bankruptcy scale of 1 to 10)

Illustration 2 ***Consolidated cash flow statement of Arvind Mills Limited for the year ended 31 st March 20X3***

(in Millions)

	Year ended March 31,20X3	Year ended March 31,20X2
A CASH FLOW FROM OPERATING ACTIVITIES		
Profit Before taxation	**2483**	**4953**
Adjustments for:		
Depreciation /Amortization	2043	1614
Others Adjustments	2363	(501)
Operating Profit before Working Capital Changes	**6892**	**6066**
Working Capital Changes:		
Changes in Inventories	(3121)	648
Changes in trade payables	2058	(92)
Changes in other current liabilities	1245	407
Changes in provisions	95	33
Changes in loans and advances	(464)	(580)
Changes in trade receivables	(1131)	(1431)
Changes in Other assets	(449)	(787)
Changes in Other Bank Balances	67	(72)
Net Changes in Working Capital	**(1700)**	**(1874)**
Cash Generated from Operations	**5192**	**4191**
Direct Taxes paid (Net of Income Tax refund)	(620)	(839)
Net Cash Flow from Operating Activities (A)	**4573**	**3352**
B CASH FLOW FROM INVESTING ACTIVITIES		
Purchase of tangible/intangible assets	(3683)	(4493)
Sale of tangible assets	665	1181

(Contd.)

Illustration 2 *(Contd.)*

Sale of Land held for sale	203	988
Changes in Investments	(281)	136
Capital Advances	125	(145)
Changes in Loans given	(422)	144
Dividend Income	4	3
Interest Income	81	71
Net cash flow before Extra Ordinary Item	**(3308)**	**(2116)**
Proceeds from Sale of Investment in Joint Venture		**2450**
Net cash flow from Investing Activities (B)	(3308)	335
C CASH FLOW FROM FINANCING ACTIVITIES		
Issue of Share Capital		2
Securities Premium received		1
Dividend Paid	(256)	
Dividend Distribution Tax Paid	(42)	
Changes in long term Borrowings	2215	(1692)
Changes in short term borrowings	1038	1020
Interest Paid	(3014)	(2947)
Net Cash flow from Financing Activities (C)	**(59)**	**(3615)**
Net Increase/(Decrease) in cash & cash equivalents (A+B+C)	**1205**	**72**
Cash & Cash equivalents at the beginning of the period	409	337
Cash & Cash equivalents at the end of the period	1614	409

Analysis 2 *Statement of Cash Flow Analysis of Arvind Limited (FY20X2–X3 compared to FY 20X1)*

	FY 20X3	FY 20X2	FY 20X1
What are the Major Sources of Cash during the period?	Operations (457) Net Borrowings (325) Sale of Fixed Assets (87)	Operations (335) Sale of Fixed Assets (217) Proceeds from Investments (280)	
What are the Major Uses of Cash during the period?	Capex (356) Cash Balance Up (121) Purchase of Investments (62) Dividends (30) Interest Paid (301)	Capex (464) Loans Repaid (67) Interest Paid (295)	

(Contd.)

Analysis 2 *(Contd.)*

	FY 20X3	FY 20X2	FY 20X1
How does the Cash Flow from Operations (CFO) compare to Net Profit figures of the firm?	CFO > 0; CFO > Net Income Due to, - Depreciation 204 - A/P & other CL items Up 330 But, - Inventories Up 312 - A/R & other CA items Up 200	CFO > 0; CFO < Net Income Due to, - Depreciation 161 - Inventories Down 65 But, - A/R Up 143 - Other CA Items Up 144	-
Is the Cash From Operations > Capex? **Is the Capex > Deprecation?**	Yes, Capex (356) > Depreciation (204)	Yes, Capex (464) > Depreciation (161)	
Is the Cash From Operations > Capex + Interest Paid + Dividend Paid? **If Yes, then where was the Excess Cash Invested?** **If No, then what are the Sources of Cash for payment of Dividends + Interest Paid + Capex**	No, Dividend Paid	No, No Dividend	
Excess Cash Invested	NA	NA	
Sources of Cash for Dividends + Interest Paid + Capex	Net Borrowings	Sale of Investments	
Other Items		Cash Balance Up (7)	
Trends **Income Before Tax**	Decreasing, Halved (190)	Increasing, Good Jump (407)	Increasing, Good Jump (176)

(Contd.)

Analysis 2 ***(Contd.)***

	FY 20X3	FY 20X2	FY 20X1
CFO **Capex** **Dividends** **Net Borrowing** **Working Capital**	Increasing, Decently (457) Decreasing, Steady State (356) Dividends Started (30) Net Borrower (325) Increased, All CA Use, CL Source	Increasing, Marginally (335) Increasing, Good Jump (464) No Dividends Net Repayer (67) No change, A/R & others use, Inventory source	Decreasing (306) Increasing, Decently (251) No Dividends Net Borrower (18) Increased, All CA Use, CL Source, Huge Inventory Jump

This company seems to be in a steady state. Operating Cash Flows are steadily improving. However, the biggest worry is the *new loans* the firm has taken in the latest year. Perhaps, the company wants to increase its size using banker's money – while, this ought to be good news – however its *high existing interest payments* is a negative signal. Shareholders have been rewarded after a long time by way of dividends. (Rating: 5.5, on a Bankruptcy scale of 1 to 10)

After going through discussion and also the wide range of illustrations, we can come to the conclusion that a *Cash Flow Statement* shows the actual flow of cash (liquidity) of the company between the two balance sheet dates. Both the Balance Sheet and the Profit & Loss Statement fail to reflect the same and thus its special significance. By forecasting future cash flows and gauging the future liquidity position of the company, a company can arrange for any shortfall in money by making arrangements in advance; and for the excess that it has, it can earn extra returns out if idle funds.

Summary

In this book, we developed the idea of flows of funds within the organization. Starting with the funds requirement for an organization, we traced the sources and uses of funds.

We have tried to study the important sources of funds, namely the funds generated from operations, sale of fixed assets, long-term borrowings and issue of new capital. Similarly, important uses of funds were traced to acquisition of fixed assets, payment of dividends, repayment of loans and capital etc. The whole exercise reveals the areas in which, funds are deployed and the sources from which, they are obtained. We also learned how to go about constructing the fund flow statement with the help of published accounting information.

We then looked at the various advances made by accounting bodies on the flow of funds. It was identified that a stand-alone fund flow statement had shortcomings in providing a few insights into a business entity's present and future financial position, especially from the liquidity perspective. The discussion then pointed out that a statement of cash flow does away with these shortcomings in a fund flow statement. Finally, we also learned about the statement of cash flow and its preparation. Using multiple illustrations, we analyzed a few statements of cash flow from real life.

Exercises

1. Multiple Choice Questions

A. Which of the following are uses of funds?
   (a) Purchase of fixed assets
   (b) Repayment of long-term loans
   (c) New issue of share capital
   (d) Only (a) and (b).

B. The important internal sources of funds are:
   (a) Funds generated from operations
   (b) Sale of non-current assets
   (c) Existing surplus working capital
   (d) None of the above.

C. Interest received on long-term investments made or on a part of non-current assets should be considered as an:
   (a) Operating activity
   (b) Investing activity
   (c) Financing activity
   (d) None of the above

D. Which of the following is a source of funds?
   (a) Issue of share capital
   (b) Sale of fixed assets or long-term investments
   (c) Non-trading receipts
   (d) Funds from operations
   (e) All of the above

E. Payment of interest on loans and dividends is classified as a:
   (a) Operating activity
   (b) Investing activity

(c) Financing activity
(d) None of the above.

F. Tinkle Comics Limited paid income tax on capital gains resulting from disposal of capital assets. This amount would be shown in the statement of cash flow as a deduction in ______ type of activities:
(a) Operating activities
(b) Investing activities
(c) Financial activities
(d) None of the above

G. Farista Financial Services Limited, a non-banking financial services company, made a total loan of ₹ 136 Crore during the financial year 20X3. This amount will be classified as part of:
(a) Operating activities
(b) Investing activities
(c) Financial activities
(d) None of the above

H. Dividend paid is always classified as a:
(a) Operating activity
(b) Investing activity
(c) Financing activity
(d) None of the above.

I. The term 'cash' as used in Cash Flow Statements includes:
(a) Only cash balances.
(b) Only bank balances.
(c) Bank balances and bank overdrafts.
(d) Cash in hand plus bank balances less bank overdrafts.
(e) All of the above.

J. Cash payments or receipts to acquire or dispose fixed assets are classified as:
(a) Operating activity
(b) Investing activity
(c) Financing activity
(d) None of the above.

2. Answer the following by completing the blank.

A. An increase in the following items can be a source of funds:

(a) ______
(b) ______
(c) ______

B. An increase in the following items can be a use of funds:
(a) ______
(b) ______
(c) ______

C. A decrease in the following items can be a use of funds:
(a) ______
(b) ______
(c) ______

D. A decrease in the following items can be a source of funds:
(a) ______
(b) ______
(c) ______

E. Change in Working Capital = Sources of Funds – ______.

F. Working Capital = Total Current Assets – ______.

3. (a) Indicate which of the following transactions would result in a (a) Source of Funds; OR (b) Use of Funds; OR (c) Neither Source nor Use of funds.

A. Amount transferred to provision for taxation
B. Collection from debtors
C. Conversion of debentures into preference shares
D. Goods sold on credit
E. Income tax refund
F. Issue of debentures
G. Issue of shares in exchange of fixed assets
H. Long term loan from bank
I. Provision created for depreciation
J. Redemption of debentures
K. Repayment of loan
L. Sale of old machinery
M. Issue of employee stock options
N. Announcement of a Bonus
O. Converting of Employee Stock Options to Equity Shares
P. Payment of tax

Q. Provision for warranties
R. Announcement of a large cash dividend
S. Redemption to preference shares
T. Announcement of a expansion plan
U. Sale of land
V. Merger with a sister concern by exchange of shares
W. Purchase of a competitors shares
X. Payment of a VRS package to an employee
Y. Loss of inventory (due to theft)
Z. Discounting of notes receivable and other receivables

4. Mark whether the following statements are "True" or "False" by marking T or F opposite each statement.

A. Funds flow is used to refer to changes in or movement of current assets and current liabilities.
B. Sources of Funds + Application of Funds = Change in working capital.
C. Investment in fixed assets is required to expand the capacity or to improve the current facilities for operation.
D. Fund requirements vary with the nature and type of business.
E. Working capital requirements are indirectly influenced by the sales volume.
F. The length of the operating cycle will influence the need for funds.
G. Shorter the duration of the operating cycle, more is the need for net working capital.
H. Funds from operations are also known as trading profits.
I. Issue of debentures is an example of application of fund.
J. The funds flow statement helps in assessing the capacity of the entity to meet its long term obligations.
K. Redemption of preference shares is an example of sources of funds.
L. Disposal of real estate is an operating activity.
M. A cash flow statement takes items according to the cash basis of accounts.
N. Dividend received in case of financial enterprises is an operating activity.

5. Analyze cash flow statement of Raymond limited (given bellow) as we have analyzed Hindustan Unilever limited and Vishnu Chemical in chapter 7.

Table 1 ***Consolidated cash flow statement of Raymond Limited for the year ended 31st March 20X3***

(in Millions)

	Year ended March 31,20X3	Year ended March 31,20X2
A. Cash Flow arising from Operating Activities:		
Net Profit before Tax and exceptional items as per Statement of Profit and Loss	**656**	**2044**
Depreciation and Amortization Expense	1890	1658
Others Adjustments	1433	1113
Operating Cash Profit before Working Capital Changes	**3985**	**4816**
Add/(Deduct):		
a) Increase in Trade and Other Payables	1579	589
b) Increase in Trade and Other Receivables	(1275)	(1370)
c) Increase in Inventories	(306)	(1315)
	(2)	(2096)
Cash Inflow from Operations	3983	2720
Deduct: Direct Taxes/Refunds (Net)	(357)	(416)
Net Cash Inflow in the course of Operating Activities	3627	2305
Deduct: Exceptional Items (Net)	371	
Net Cash Inflow in the course of Operating Activities after exceptional items (A)	**3256**	**2305**
B. Cash Flow arising from Investing Activities:		
Inflow:		
a) Sale of Fixed Assets	103	232
b) Interest Received	120	101
c) Dividend Received	78	154
d) Sale of Non-Current Investments	5	306
e) Sale of Current Investments (Net)	182	
	489	793

(Contd.)

Table 1 ***(Contd.)***

	Year ended March 31,20X3	Year ended March 31,20X2
Outflow:		
a) Acquisition of Fixed Assets	2103	2461
b) Acquisition of Minority Interest	2	
c) Investment in Subsidiary		186
d) Purchase of Current Investments (Net)		121
	2105	2768
Net Cash Outflow in the course of Investing Activities (B)	**(1616)**	**(1975)**
C. Cash Flow arising from Financing Activities:		
Inflow:		
a) Proceeds from Long Term Loans (Net)	78	
b) Proceeds from other Borrowings (Net)	254	1619
	332	1619
Outflow:		
a) Repayment of Borrowings (Net)		349
b) Finance Charges (Net)	1759	1516
c) Dividend Paid	178	71
	1938	1936
Net Cash Outflow in the course of Financing Activities (C)	**(1606)**	**(316)**
D. Change in Currency Fluctuation Reserve arising on consolidation	**(18)**	**14**
Net Increase in Cash and Cash Equivalents (A+B+C)	16	27
Add: Balance at the beginning of the year	308	264
Less : Cash and Cash Equivalents transferred upon Acquisition of subsidiary		17
Cash and Cash Equivalents at the close of the year	**324**	**308**

Keys

1.

A. (d)

B. (a), (b), and (c) all three

C. (b)

D. (e)
E. (c)
F. (b)
G. (a)
H. (c)
I. (d)
J. (b)

2.

A.
- (a) New issue of share capital
- (b) New issue of bonds
- (c) Sale proceeds of fixed assets

B.
- (a) Funds lost in operation
- (b) Redemption of debentures
- (c) Purchase of fixed assets

C.
- (a) Account payable
- (b) Short term loans
- (c) Tax provisions

D.
- (a) Inventories
- (b) Fixed assets
- (c) Investments

E. Application of Funds
F. Total Current Liabilities

3.

A. Amount transferred to provision for taxation – (a)
B. Collection from debtors – (a)
C. Conversion of debentures into preference shares – (c)
D. Goods sold on credit – (a)
E. Income tax refund – (a)
F. Issue of debentures – (a)
G. Issue of shares in exchange of fixed assets – (c)
H. Long term loan from bank – (a)

I. Provision created for depreciation – (a)
J. Redemption of debentures – (b)
K. Repayment of loan – (b)
L. Sale of old machinery – (a)
M. Issue of employee stock options – (c)
N. Announcement of a Bonus – (c)
O. Converting of Employee Stock Options to Equity Shares – (a)
P. Payment of Tax – (b)
Q. Provision for warranties – (a)
R. Announcement of a large cash dividend – (c)
S. Redemption to Preference Shares – (b)
T. Announcement of an expansion plan – (c)
U. Sale of land – (a)
V. Merger with sister concern by exchange of shares –(c)
W. Purchase of a competitors shares – (b)
X. Payment of a VRS package to an employee – (b)
Y. Loss of inventory (due to theft) – (b)
Z. Discounting of notes receivable and other receivables – (a)

4.

A. T
B. F
C. T
D. T
E. F
F. T
G. F
H. T
I. F
J. F
K. F
L. F
M. T
N. T

5.

Table1 Analysis ***Statement of Cash Flow Analysis of Raymond Limited (FY20X2–X3 compared to FY 20X1)***

	FY 20X3	FY 20X2	FY 20X1
What are the Major Sources of Cash during the period?	Operations (326) Net Borrowings (33) Income from Investments/Sale (29) Sale of Fixed Assets (10)	Operations (230) Net Borrowings (127) Income from Investments/Sale (44) Sale of Fixed Assets (23)	
What are the Major Uses of Cash during the period?	Capex (210) Finance Charges (176) Dividend (18)	Capex (265) Finance Charges (152) Dividend (7)	
How does the Cash Flow from Operations (CFO) compare to Net Profit figures of the firm?	CFO > 0; CFO > Net Income CFO up due to - Depreciation (189) - A/P Up (158) But, - A/R Up (127) - Inventories Up (31)	CFO > 0; CFO > Net Income CFO up due to - Depreciation (166) - A/P Up (59) But, - A/R Up (137) - Inventories Up (131)	-
Is the Cash From Operations > Capex? **Is the Capex > Deprecation?**	Yes Capex (210) > Depreciation (189)	Yes Capex (265) > Depreciation (166)	
Is the Cash From Operations > Capex + Interest Paid + Dividend Paid? **If Yes, then where was the Excess Cash Invested?** **If No, then what are the Sources**	No, Dividend Increased	No, Dividend Paid	

(*Contd.*)

Table 1 Analysis ***(Contd.)***

	FY 20X3	FY 20X2	FY 20X1
of Cash for payment of Dividends + Interest Paid + Capex			
Excess Cash Invested	NA	NA	
Sources of Cash for Dividends + Interest Paid + Capex	Net Borrowings	Net Borrowings	
Other Items	Increase in Cash Balance 2	Increase in Cash Balance 3	
Trends **Income Before Tax** **CFO** **Capex** **Dividends** **Net Borrowing** **Working Capital**	Decreasing, Steep Fall (66) Increasing, Steadily (326) Decreasing, Consolidating (210) Increasing, Steadily (18) Net Borrower (33) Improved, All CA Use, CL Source	Increasing, Marginally (204) Increasing, Good Jump (230) Increasing, Decently (265) Started Paying (7) Net Borrower (127) Increased, All CA Use, CL Source	Good Turnaround (194) Decreasing (59) Increasing, Consolidating (138) No Dividends Net Repayer (43) Mild Improvement, Not Much

Overall Assessment of the company is that it is slowly and steadily consolidating. Operating Cash Flows are steadily improving. However, the *past leverage* is acting as a bottle neck for the management as most of the income earned goes in *payment of interest to the bankers*. Good news is the shareholders have started getting rewarded – though modestly. Working capital indicates steady trends of consolidation and leveraging its market power. (Rating: 6.5 on a Bankruptcy scale of 1 to 10)

Index

A
Accounts payable, 33
Accounts receivables, 17
Amortization, 26, 36
Arvind Limited, 81, 76

B
Balancing figure, 11

C
CAPEX, also Capital Expenditure, 45, 61n
Capital Requirements, 21, 88
Cash, 1-2, 15
Cash Flow Cycle, 32
Cash payments, 19, 62
Cash receipts, 10, 61, 62
Current Assets, 4, 18, 24
Current Liabilities, 4, 42, 72

D
Debt, 55, 59
Debtors, 17
Depreciation, 12n, 22, 23n, 26
  Straight line method, 8

F
Financing activities, 48, 58-59, 61
Fixed Assets, 18, 32
Funds, 3-4, 24-25, 27
Fund Flow Statement, 3, 34-35, 43-44, 49

H
Hindustan Unilever Limited, 61, 65

I
Intangible assets, 24, 26
Inventory, 11n, 29, 33
  Raw material, 18, 28
  Work in Progress, 18, 28
  Finished goods, 18, 28
Investing activities, 48, 58-59

J
Jump investments, 19

L
Long term loans, 24
Long term liability, 11n

N
Net current assets, 6
Net working capital, 4, 6, 28
Non-current assets, 18, 48
Non-current debt, 24

O
Operating Activities, 48, 58-59
  Direct method, 50, 51, 62
  Indirect method, 50, 51, 62
Operating Cycle, 4-5, 29, 32

P
Provogue Limited, 76-78

R
Raymond Limited, 89, 93
Receivables, 16-17, 62, 80
Retained Earnings, 15

S
Sundry debtors, 17

T
Total Current Assets, 4
Trading income, 35
Trading profits, 35

W
Working capital, 3-4, 6, 8, 14, 17, 19, 24

Authors' Profiles

Dr. N. Ramachandran is the Director of Kochi Business School, Kochi, Kerala. An MBA and Ph.D. from and a fellow of IIM Calcutta. Dr. Ramachandran has over three decades of academic experience at his alma mater and Asian Institute of Technology (AIT), Bangkok, where he was also the Chief Internal Auditor. He has been a consultant to government and non-government agencies in various countries, including India, Thailand, Laos, Sri Lanka, Cambodia and Vietnam. His area of interest includes Financial Structure of Industries, Corporate Financial Accounting and Strategic Cost Management.

Dr. Ram Kumar Kakani is currently a Professor at XLRI – Xavier School of Management, Jamshedpur, India, with a past corporate experience. A fellow of IIM Calcutta, Dr. Kakani has been a resident academician at international institutions in Copenhagen, Dubai, Lagos and Singapore and has conducted research with the support of Aditya Birla Research Centre (ABRC) of the London Business School and National Stock Exchange of India. A recipient of the AIMS Best Young Teacher Award (2005) and ranked among the top 1% of the Social Science Research Network (SSRN) authors. His area of interest includes Accounting Analysis, Corporate Finance, Corporate Strategy, and Study of Business Groups.